# THE COLLECTED POEMS OF KAY BOYLE

# COLLECTED POEMS OF
# KAY BOYLE

COPPER CANYON PRESS / PORT TOWNSEND

ISBN 1-55659-038-5 (Cloth)
ISBN 1-55659-039-3 (Paper)
Library of Congress Catalog Card Number 90-85089

The publication of this book was supported by a grant from the National Endowment for the Arts.

Copper Canyon Press is in residence with Centrum at Fort Worden State Park.

COPPER CANYON PRESS
Post Office Box 271
Port Townsend, Washington 98368

# PUBLISHER'S NOTE

This book includes all the poems of Kay Boyle. Her first volume, *Landscape for Wyn Henderson,* was published in London by Curwen Press in 1931. Her first U.S. edition, *A Statement,* was published in 1932 by Modern Editions Press of New York. She continued to revise some poems and included them with new work in *A Glad Day* (New Directions, 1938); *American Citizen Naturalized in Leadville, Colorado* (Simon and Schuster, 1944); *Collected Poems* (Knopf, 1962); *Testament for My Students and Other Poems* (Doubleday, 1970); and *This Is Not a Letter and Other Poems* (Sun & Moon Press, 1985). For this edition, poems are presented in roughly chronological order. Many of the poems were dated during the compilation of Ms. Boyle's *Collected Poems* in 1970. Others, including revised and undated poems, are placed according to most recent publication, with new poems presented last. Thanks are due to Ms. Boyle's son, Ian Franckenstein, and to her biographer, Sandra Whipple Spanier, for their assistance.

# TABLE OF CONTENTS

TO SHAWN WONG

# MOTHERS

In the still of night
Have we wept.
And our hearts, shattered and aching
Have prayed.
In the cold, cold moonlight
Have we sobbed
And dreamed of what might have been.
And our hearts have bled from stabs
Given unheeding.
We are the women who have suffered alone —
Alone and in silence.

(1917)

# THE BATTLEFIELD

The gray night falls
And rises high some smoke –
A black, black line against the sky.
A white star shines from out the mists
And smiles upon the bleeding hearts of men.

(copybook 1 9 1 6 – 1 9 1 8 )

# THE PEOPLE'S CRY

Great King, there is no hatred in this heart for you,
There is no anger in my soul.
Only a man's deep pity for a brother,
Do I feel, only a wish that you could understand.
We fought, Great King, for what you thought was right —
We were the puppets and you pulled the strings.
We did not know for what we fought —
'Twas to protect our honor, so you said, and we our souls aflame,
Answered the trumpets' call.
Honor — what does it mean?
Does it mean a bloody war?
Is not *our* honor greater, higher than this, O King?
Higher than death and destruction, highest above all?
Is not to protect our honor to stand, wondrous and fine,
Helping those countries about to grow as we have done?
Is not honor a marvelous love and a heart that holds all men?
King, that's what we call honor, and you we feel are wrong.
But if you *are* right and honor *is* death and hate and kill,
If the honor we fight for is stained by a brother's blood —
King, we would rather die in the fight,
Die rather than see our children rejoice in the fact
That we murdered our brothers so.
But King, because you have said it,
Our children will think it right
That we fought "to protect our honor,"
So King, we die in the fight.

(copybook 1916 – 1918)

# IN DEFENSE OF HOMOSEXUALITY

I speak of it as a thing with a future
At present badly done by amateurs neglecting
An opportunity to be discriminating

It being an occupation in itself
It should not be confused with reticence
Or the perceptions of a shy man
Nor should it be segregated on a question of morality

To fit the part the incentive
Must be more than casual
Rather a weakness at the very roots
An appetite which leaves one flat, an inability
To get into the dirt, thread worms upon a hook,
Wash a floor clean; a vacancy
Which cannot read a page without a recognition
Of the symmetry of the thumb lying along it;
A similarity of gesture as professional as the whore's
And to the tough taste as flavorless
The loyalties of such are more perishable
Than the crust of an egg

A dislike of sweat and odor, of blowing the nose,
Of raising children clears the emotions to the hem of the garment only.
( O how sacred is the hem of thy garment hem of thy eyelid hem of thy hem
O how sacred art thou to me thou delicate-veined thou wild boy.
Benvenuto swathed in silks the limbs of his fresh one his virgin
And the boy went among the women as a girl and made free with them
And then told them that he was with child
And the women did lay their compassionate hands upon his belly
And upon his limbs and upon the flesh of his thighs
In commiseration, and then were their hearts rended with sweet anguish
And with terror as the rod blossomed in their fingers. )

By incentive is meant that fidelity to purpose
Which determines one to hold a parasol
Over tomato plants to shield them from the elements.

I prefer a rabbit neatly killed (to serve a purpose not create one)
Who under the knife blade peels like a ripe fig
The skin while still warm ripped in a piece from the royal satin flesh
Which it has lipped with intimate tenacity
Such a caress is worth a generation of these indecisions
We are asked to accept as celebrations of a genuine passion

Nor does this signify that man cannot be to man a complement
Rather than a reflection of his own devices
Or that one might surprise those generosities, not of the mind
But richer, warmer than, which women find it imperative
(But no less valid) to make use of.
Nor does this state an apprehension placing
Women as women, men as fairies with a finality
That permits no accident

A cat is initiated by his mother's lovers
A necessary preamble to the method and satisfaction of fathering kittens.
The human proceeds in the reverse direction
Establishing a home, hearth, fireside within those organs
Which respond like blind men to a lick of fire.
Put under glass some of them could be worn as cameos
Their femininity plumbed to the depths of
A tedious vocation as engrossing as bee-raising
And as monotonous to the outsider.

(1925)

# CAREER

there are many ways now of being a young man
not so simple as ploughing a field
spading a black patch
        strung thick with earthworms
or making love
a procession of lace handkerchiefs
swept up from lawns
      floors
           checkerboards

I would be finding a new way
to bend water making a fan of it
to chill the desert
brand cattle   break horses with
           the pulse of the knee
     Spring nights would catch me
horning new timber down salmon-rivers
my breath at lonely corners linger all night
         with whiskey-singing
sun cracking whips upon my skin of hard man
speech running sweet
     raw
        high
           under the hay

(1926)

# HUNT

The buckhounds went on under the rain
with the wet fern swinging lace over their eyes
and their skins hanging like crumpled velvet

the bucks shod with leaves like silk sandals
danced on chopsticks over the suey of red lizards
        white stalks
        and caterpillars

the gentlemen slapped with their crop-butts at their clean leather

Now the gentlemen turn back out of the high dripping world
to fires that repeat themselves in the copper
of andirons and whiskey glasses

with the throats of the buckhounds sunk over their insteps
and the hound teats bruised blue on the fine floor

                      (1926)

# TO AMERICA

How shall I come to you with this to say to you,
With soft steps saying hush in the leaves or with anger,
To say that a wind dies down in an old country,
That a storm makes rain grow like white wheat on the sand.

How shall I say there is no desert except beyond him
And that your soil is rich dark banners flying under the plow;
That the clay of his bones is a hard famine
And the taste of his words is strange, strange to the tongue.

To remember is to see goats on the hills with spring in their nostrils,
To see ripples laid sharp as shells at a thin prow;
To cry Now let there be words to come, let there be pillars of song to set over
    him,
Let the rain fall in fresh caverns
And roots weave the earth with trumpets of sound.

There shall be full years and you will not need him,
But in years lean as the locust you shall listen in the crops for him
And he will be there.
He is a full swinging river that has always flowed for you,
His footsteps are wild valleys thundering down under your hills.

He will be a long time in your blood.
He will be a long time coming again to you.
You shall try to gather his seed when it is blown far from the stalk.
If ever you comb the wind for him, or turn the earth for a flavor of him,
Night will have fitted a cold armor to him:
There will be flutes of stone and javelins at his fingers
And before him a wild clear sea clanging for war.

(1926)

# FOR AN AMERICAN

*for E. W.*

I

You are the scorched columns, the green nave which struck thirteen times by lightning continues to thrust mon chevalier Saint Michel into the clouds. Below you, the windows are pleated in the Roman stone: blades of green grass hung with fine moss and delicate bouquets of lichen. . . .

You have danced with your hard feet backward, as in Indian dances, through the dry stalks and the silver milk-pods which tapped at the cups of your knees; over burnt ground and devastation, through bush of hard bloodless berry where no other vegetation could survive; over soil closed like a fist about the roots of flowers; over violence and dry rot; under grapes gone to powder in their fine skins.

Not plumes of the sea did you offer, but gaunt feathers, bare rigging of ships, desert foliage, wind like metal in the nostrils, wind dark, rich, sweet in the mouth.

Who shall say I have not known you if I have sat with the pillars of the church growing about me, air thin as glass and stones like firm lids upon my eyes? I have seen the bronze statue seven times larger than a sheep above the refectory whose windows open like a silk fan, and the black saint reeling with clouds, dripping with vines of fresh rain. I have seen the candles lit at the altar's prow, so simple that the carving became a desecration; and the shadows of the church rising and breaking on pure cones of candle-foam. . .


and you like a candle lit at the extremity of the ermine sleeve: a bright wing in the night, a flame bleached out in the sun.

There is no wilderness in America as savage. None with the tough bark of the trees as black, and the flowers solid and sweet between the teeth. Nowhere else does flesh become to the eye as odor in the nostril.

Under the stripped trees the earth of this country lies in strong furrows. The tongue of the plow carves avenues of loam. Spring nineteen-twenty-six and the soft bodies of moles lying like small black panthers in the trail of the horses' feet. Only here is the earth among the roots of the trees printed with toad feet, needled with moss, dark and inseparable about the fine bones of the fern.

There is this then to set between the bitter cold and the summer. This to return to and discover like new leaves at that season: spring, and his hair falling two ways on his forehead; tassels of fresh rain, and his mouth.

III

Death is a hand under the chin lifting the eyes to set again at the core
The petals that have fallen into the caverns of men's voices,
The loose ends of sound that are slow hoofs passing with hair swinging slow
    at the fetlock,
Stroking soft hides and haunches and proud necks arched to the darkness —
To make a music rich deep strong enough to rouse you,
To lead armies bitter enough to serve you,
With cries of beasts on the wind like the shattering of fresh bells.

Dolphin-wing in the wind, wind in the wing with the sea falling,
Night is a full-feathered fan to cool you.
Ah, turn now and hear them: sound, color, and taste making a strong way to
    you!
Do not be dead, take all that is gentle and warm to you;
Turn now to the warm mouths to embrace, the hot wine red in veins and the
    glasses,
And this heart, this heart in the breast shriveling like a burning flower.

There is a miracle in the hot road and the long slow heat of the sea in the
    open window.
How else have the heavy hills fallen among the geranium leaves and the
    coarse stems of the plant?
Or how could the sea move thick in my blood and the dust rise?
There is a small clear sea between us in which anemone, sea-plants and
    petals move and ripple and stir murmuring.
Through the pale fans of the fish and the weaving weed
There is a sea laid like a small cool hand between us.


### LAMENT

Here I sit quiet and blind in the sun
With new leaves coming wet on the boughs in the light
And in darkness and the dark sap singing
    Aaron, Aaron, I would be a great tree over you
    Aaron, I would be air running like a sea in your nostrils

The wind is a shawl drawn on the points of my shoulders
Shaking loose in the wind with me, the sky is split on the chimneys
        and
    Aaron, I would be a dark valley curved to cradle you
    Aaron, I would be a thin vessel to bear you a fierce wine
    To tables where dry bread is eaten
    Aaron, Aaron, I would be a soft word in your mouth
    When the cold comes to shatter your bones

(1926)

# AND WINTER

This night is a bitter cry for you
it is a dark cry for you
held hollow to your ear in the cavern of my heart
Dark and impenetrable as the wings of deep valleys
my blood is a long lament for you
The dry twigs of the winter willow
rub their lean bones against the glass

Orion fades like the white heel of a runner
and my anguish is as bitter as almond rind
My hands in the underbrush of my sorrow
like children seek the new vines of arbutus
that run in winter like music under the leaves

Here is the sweet wine of my knees to be poured for you
my temples are hollow bowls for the fruit of your mouth
The waves of the sea pace the shore and bemoan you
They cry out and wring their white hands in anguish
  Stir in me cool as the pulse of the wind
  lie in my veins and chill and chill me
  Until the blood runs cold through my heart

(1926)

# CARNIVAL 1927

She is a grotesque
He would pass her by in the street this winter
Seeing the drum before her
And the bouquets of yellow rice thrown in her hair
Her breasts
        wear little blue veils of veins to mask them
This is her costume    This was the way of finding
A queer shape for herself

This year he is not in the streets
        after the red heels of the maple
His arm is not the gay arm around the soft waists of the girls

He is cold as a tide of flesh cooling
        when the blood halts in the body
And the lean steps of the heart fall one by one

The curtain shakes all night in the window
Like a fan at the cold embers
    Scarecrow
        hung-man in the wind
Stop rattling your bones at that white crow the moon

# A LETTER TO FRANCIS PICABIA

There is one country
      and no shame to it
For having a heart hot in the bosom
Or songs in the mouth humming
That servant-girls sing at their dishes
Wherever the men of it are
Are the laughter and the sorrowing
      of their own land
And whenever a stranger speaks
it is an odd word he is saying

The rich coins sing in the hands of them
But whether it is I am deaf now
Or whether it is I am blinded
By the thought of the dead
      rank in my eyes even
I am weary
      for speech like new cress in the river
I am sick for a sight of him
      for whom my tears fall

## II

I ask more of this season
Than leaves seeking the ground
      birds guiding the wind south
      or a doorstep swept clean for winter
No lost things
      fingers of stars pointing out
      steps on the wet grass
      the moon ringing the hay-bells the frogs crying
      out upon what a mouth said or remembered
Or the eyelids of one town lifting
      No answer

From fields struck dumb with frost
But a new season blooming
        a new history of feast-days
For a young man who died one autumn

III

If I thought
        this is the way I'd be
Waiting when the door
        let him in
        lock of hair blown on the room's face
I'd be combing it
        back of my ears if I
Thought he'd be growing up in the glass
this is the way my legs
        crossed and my hands
                        lying
If I thought I could
        see him make sugars fly
up his cuffs after dinner find
        potatoes hot in the dogs' ears
if I thought I could
        hear the thin bark of
his shoes on the gravel this is the way
        my eyes waiting
and my heart crying until
        I be dead with him

(1927)

# O THIS IS NOT SPRING

O this is not spring but in me
        there is a murmuring of new things
This is the time of a dark winter in the heart
        but in me are green traitors

The dead lie apart with their throats laid full with sorrow
And the blood of the living moves slow in the cold
There is no one
To play the street like a flute with me
For a return on the old footsteps

They say write to me how the snow falls this winter
And if the horse sets out well on the road
And I answer
This year the blood cannot lie quiet
And the sun goes swift, swift through the hair

(1927)

# A CHRISTMAS CAROL
# FOR EMANUEL CARNEVALI

This year I have sent you
A small chocolate heart entirely surrounded
By roses carved in sugar
In the middle there are two hands in paper
Clasped with a yellow charm at the wristbone
In the veins of it there is a music running
Of days spread like peacock tails
Of days worn savagely like parrot feathers

I believe that the truth should be spoken but if it be questions you are asking answer that in youth the day is so full that the voice swells loud and wide to surround it and with age does the day wear thin like an old beast boned with pain; answer that the years run through the fingers and the trees set aside their leaves as if they were tears falling

Ask that the wind rattle sleep to a heart that turns and turns in its own anguish, shuddering and smoldering it to ashes stirred by the wind; that winter be softened by flames that leap like horned stags in the chimney: not a man scarred with the cold, tied stiff by it, frozen with his own water fallen fanwise upon a wall where lizards no longer burrow for shade and slumber with grains of sand fallen in yellow stars between their claws

Behind us lie nights feathered with sleep, the mouth saluting feet swifter than gulls. Next year I shall make you a carpet of many small faces, the petals of almond flowers, with temples split on the tip of a chianti sunset: and land like a child's ear lying open for speech to whittle and pierce it.

## THE LEGEND

There were two men as fine as wild beasts, and as wild, with silky coats and tongues as red as satin, who set out to cross the snow, leaping and sporting together like young dogs in the cold. They had not gone far, with the memory of their own hearths still burning in them, when they came upon a traveler who, like a scarecrow fallen among white sheaves of wheat, had dropped in his own steps in the snow. He was an old man and as the two fell upon their knees beside him to lift up his hands and his head in order to breathe upon his flesh, they could see the scars and the blemishes which time had laid upon his skin.

They had kneeled down by his side and emptied their mouths in blasts of sweet breath upon his neck and his palms, but in his veins they could perceive no stirring of life, and not only did their breathing upon him fail to revive him, but the breaths themselves strangely enough floated away in pure little halos as perfectly formed as the rings which hang about the necks of doves.

As they chafed his hands between their own and sought upon their persons for warm drinks with which to thaw the saps of his body, they were filled with a fear and a dismay of this man's flesh. On the back of his hands sprung thin forests of gray entangled hairs which grew thicker upon his wrists and his forearms, and in his neck were scars illy-sewn in angry welts, and his great ears were planted with stained gray ferns of hair.

They looked upon him, and as they looked into each other's faces over the stiff flesh of the old man, they were aware of their own beautiful bodies, clean and without blemish in their clothing. And then they let fall his hands from their own and they made haste to be off and so abandon him to the ferocity of his own dying.

But as they fled over the snow from where the old man was lying, their shadows pursued them as if with evil intent, and their hearts began to smite them. One thought: "Were I to give this old man my fair hands and the beauty of my arms to bear him, then to be sure I could save him from death." And the other thought: "Were I to bestow upon him all the fire of my limbs and the wits of my clear mind, these gifts would surely bring him to shelter and spare him for many long years to come." And thus they went on, questioning and chiding themselves in their own hearts.

But before long they had succumbed to the doubts which the old man's plight had stirred in them, and with ennobled and richer decision they turned upon their steps to regain his side and to bear unto him the gifts of their strength and their goodwill. But as they ran the snow fell suddenly apart before them and a youth of great beauty and gentleness emerged from the cruel ground. His feet were bared to the cold but white violets and all manner of early blossoms were springing up between his toes. With his fingers he played upon an instrument of which they had no knowledge, and to this melody of his own making he said unto them:

> Wiefor shud ye feer deth for hyme
> Ande weifer shud ye tremble
> Fer hev not I suffered that ther shud be pece in yur harts
> Ande hev not I dyed fer ye
> That ye myghte liv to a gret olde age
> Now do I aske won favore of ye
> Ande it is thet ye giv not yur beautye
> Unto thum who hev no eyes fer it
> Ande thet ye luv not thum who hev killed me

The beautiful youth struck his instrument with his fingers and he looked upon their wondering faces, and he spoke again to them:

> Won daye I shall aske of ye to giv yur blud
> Fer the lyfe of a yung lamb
> But thum who hev never looked upon me
> Giv not the breth of yur mouths to suckle thum

And as they gazed in wonder upon him, the earth closed again upon the elegant youth and the snow fell again in the same way that it had fallen, but it was as if a weight had been lifted from their hearts that he had spoken to them. So they joined hands together and continued lightly on their way. And no more thought did they give to the old man who had perished until at the change of the season they chanced to pass again by the place where he had fallen, and lo, there had grown up a great tree, and its branches spread out over them as they paused and sheltered them from a passing shower.

II

Now are there voices of children
Hard cold at the door singing
And in the blood a tide rising as if an army were stirring.
I would say that a man and his country wither
When a sea runs between them

29

But the words of my mouth take flight as I come to them
And the word of truth lies still in my heart.

Italy, contained in you
As richly as in the skin of a grape,
I would find on your tongue some flavor
On your lips some word of him.
Italy
Like opening a window upon a garden
Which need not be pruned, pathed, swept, or weeded,
A land sown with miracles
Before which the snow parts into spring,
A coast you walk drawing
The warm sea back on your shoulders
The sun down over your brows.

Here the wind has fallen in strange ways
And the vanes fly in the storm crying
East, west, to the lost elements.
I would go down
Into the towns that remember
The hills turned green again
The roads bitter with dust
I would talk of him for whom the waters fall softly.

### III

Houses are not teeth in the hill, nor claws deep in the rock's bark, but riders
got weary, dismounted to lie down at the side of the water, to touch the pine
needles and stare at their own faces. They come up out of the grass and into
the hard leather of the boughs and go off over the roads, shod feet among the
thistles and loose rock seeking the spare places and points as high needles.

Here in the north are the riders got weary, laid down with fires built at their
hearts, with mouths humming of corn-bread, of white meal, of foxfeet, with
thought of you warmer than any fuel winged in the chimney.

Now in forests and forests do the trees stand dark and sorrowing, and I say
to them that their fine limbs shall kneel to you, their nimble necks arch to

you. I say you will put in their mouths reins of light flexible as minnows, and
out, out, the dark far earth will be soft under the hoofs of the wind

     galloping
           galloping     galloping
        galloping
with nostrils like wild black pansies opened on the fog.

                             (1927)

# A CONFESSION TO EUGENE JOLAS

They have come back from Russia
With a life in them to set against
What the Jews, American Indians, the Irish even
Have succumbed to: the withering of the flower
That each man carries in his heart.
It withered in the blood of the Royal ones who went
Listlessly through Rambouillet to exile, it has gone bitter
In Jews who have found a country richer than faith was to them;
In Indians who lie quiet under the cannon
No longer biding time for the passing of swifter races;
In the Irish in whose century of black starvation
The flower bloomed more fiercely than a tropic flower.

There is a humanity now
Set upon the proud high inhumanity of architects,
An undermining pity at the roots when America builds
Considering those laws demanding that light and air be zoned
To preserve the weaker ones
(How many men died for Athens
Did Chartres consider or Mont St. Michel
The lives broken or walled-in for beauty?)
They come back in a year that has no stirs, no showers,
No days of indecision for those who bloom out of season;
No loosening of the soil of an established winter strong as Minnesota
    blizzards,
Speaking of Russia as the first men speaking of America
Cut their fervent way through wildernesses.
Or saying: it is the last spadeful of soil flung down
Upon the grave of artists; saying Russia is following
The Roman road of pragmatism with the bodies of "crucified men
Stretching for five miles along each side of it,"
Protesting that even Lenin's corpse has compromised with time.

They return disturbed
In a year when the Jews, Indians, the Irish sit quiet

And the thunder of falls is no longer heard, or of strong rivers,
Or exploration known, these things having ebbed westward with the
    savage
To oblivion, incest and death, these things having died naturally in
    degeneration.

A study of the past is the experiences of other men
Set down without complete authority, having seen them in my own time
Returning with a maybe maybe for a new country.

II

for R. McA.

O pretty papa so much have you done for me that my spirit falters
I am not waiting for tenderness to fill the kid's heart with plenty plenty of
    gratitude
under the powder the rouge the borrowed clothes I am not sitting with the
    kid on my knee
waiting a pretty papa the tender but peeled eye under the mascara
    estimating his value as a
provider to take us home and let us hang up our stockings at Christmas

but one man I see the skin of his lips and his eyes rocking
it is his filthy words on me and his sad words and his blame on me
I remember and his wireless not saying the country is beautiful I
have thought of somebody else every minute but saying I'm beginning to
    spill things
not that I've had too much to drink but too little

III

for E.J. & R S.

You carry fatherhood as it should be
a man too absorbed in his own language
to demand it of other people in the restaurant
an admiration for a little girl with white hair

you see her go come hesitate like a fly on icing
you looking sideways the way a man should
upon his wife and children always

33

talking to someone else absently observing
the ankles and breasts that go by on the sidewalk

Or you little boy with your eyes asking what
wouldn't I do to you if once I got you with no
words between us if once I skinned you clean of your
Paris markets at morning of your flair and scent for
the negroid

you think you're my idea of a night out when even my
hottest blood cannot get warm to you if we danced all
night even over the cabbages the celery and the carrots
what would be left to us in the morning but a hot day
and the nostalgia for somebody else's kisses

IV

*for M.N., R.D., M.R., J.G., H.M., H.C., B.S., M.M., H.C. Jr.*

There is nothing so beautiful as young men in fine clothes
Young men with faces shaved to rose-petals Toes pointed in patent leather
Asking so much of the back-seats of taxi-cabs
O you Frenchboys it is life to me the breath stinking of garlic
in dock bistrots, the clouds sober and the first stars rolled out like dice

Once I swam from Covington to the Ohio shore
through the white curls of the Island Queen as she churned up to Coney
        Island
carrying so much dirt on me that I smelled
like a bushy-tailed mammal for days after;
And once I wore suphur blossoms in my hair
to drive the lice away. One autumn rolled
like a dog in beds of rotting seaweed to get
the fleas off my body and the fever out of my veins

                    I have been out in the amorous night
                    oh lalito
                    and I have come home wearing the Tour Eiffel
                    like a spanish comb in my hair
                    the black river has overflowed its banks this spring

and has come into my eyes so that I am blinded with
    glamor
and entered my nostrils so that I snort like a young filly
crossing the Champs de Mars


                              v


                                        *for A.S.*
Now that the lights run out
        and the wheels and the timber of trains cry on the river
Now that there is a tide of spring rising against the prows
There is no one to come into the room and say the same honor
Marches in the wrists
                the music
                        the same blood is there


Whatever sweet stalks there are they will be withering
In the sea salted and summer a wide road under the sun
Let it be that the cold leaves the tight fists of April
Pointed and swelled but could not flower
                        this year


Mornings come like torches to strange rooms
where I have gone to bed in darkness not knowing
                if there were books
                chairs photographs
How to write of it


I had no use for it
        hating the conversation and the wallpaper
        nothing to remember
                but the turn of a head scratching
                and a man in the street singing for rabbit-hides


                        ( 1 9 2 8 )

# DEDICATED TO ROBERT McALMON

What good did your blood do you
if it gave you honey under the tongue
a deep valley for the wind to lie still in
and sent you wandering
over the dams of timber sawn white by the teeth of beavers
over the badger country for hawthorn sap
and the sight of wild onion

It would be a good thing to sit quiet
Flesh salted on the wharves and eyes clean with brine
Talking chewing and talking
To sit with the bricks swept
and the wind steady as light shafting seaward
and the hard foam clanging upon the land

It would be a good thing to return
out of the cold now the seams in the ice cracking wide
the wild heart whoring the hard eye warming
to the nest of an oriole hanging like iron grapes in a pine
Talk about the afternoon you found a young goat
and brought it home in your arms with its legs dangling
and its muzzle pressed cool and wet on your face
Eyes beckoning a sail off the cold plains that lie like priests' gowns
    discarded
and the priests themselves in their white skins
lost in the music of the waves

What good did it do you
the softness of gulls' breasts in you
and a winter as hard as any winter
that lies in an old man's heart
Buried deep so that no light of the moon
or any light can draw you
out of the corpse-soil and the quiet
out of the nights that cry like wolves in the dark

(1928)

# THE UNITED STATES

*for William Carlos Williams*

Not a land, or like other lands, with trees coming out and the grass growing,
Or of waters shriveling in the wind like the faces of old women;
But however the body turns there are days when the blood in the veins even
Flows to the north stars for warmth like the cold blood of a compass,
And nights with the birch moon drifting cold as Maine water,
And the Pleiades running like snipes' feet on the rivers.
But whatever you asked of it, not the seeking or the finding of your own
    kind
But the Indian, the silent ways of the old men you were asking;
Days with the sun worn thin as a 'coon's skin, deep creeks where salmon
    took the falls,
Coming to timber towns, the frontier and to England,
To barns where your grandmother danced with her lovers, with her young
    heels shining like white apples in the dark;
Asking of history one Englishman not watching his own shadow,
Singing a false note, limping: one Englishman blind, naked, humming it
    out of tune,
To give you a taste for horseshoes and the white eyes of miners;
Whatever you asked of it, not the mountain-kids of other countries,
To jump through the flames of bonfires, or the goats to return from the hills,
Running on their black hoofs to snuff the sugar from your palms;
Nor questions to tickle and flutter the stiff wings of the goats' ears
As they titter together and slide their coarse eyes in their faces;
Nor to go back into the hills and to see them, the beasts struck dumb in the
    bush,
Tentative, with their eyes in the darkness like the lights of tall houses,
And their tongues tasting the sweet night, and their horned teeth
    crunching the thick leaves of summer,
Nor the owls crying softly in the rain.

But to go back, to go back to another country, to go back
And to say from here I can see it;
Here and here a leaf opening, here the cherry-gum dripping,
Here a stream broken through, here and here a horse run wild.

(1928)

37

# THE ONLY BIRD THAT SANG

The church mice had been bombed out of Albert
The corporal under the gas ring
Said he would get out for good this time
If the roquefort didn't sit still on the plate
Instead of bruising its bottom green on the table.
For the French it was the way it ought to be
The roquefort but the corporal had a sore throat
And it had been raining all day

>They have planted a flower
>Under the rose trees at Albert
>Pneumonia cool as edelweiss
>Was the last thing blooming into a song for him
>Singing to him like a mama
>This century the war that came whistling
>The only bird that sang

After forty-eight hours of marriage with the elements
The corporal took out the roquefort
He had brought with him for company
It was winging in his pocket like a hummingbird
In Amiens he felt it out saying soit sage to it
In Albert he saw the gangrene on it was eating closer
And closer to the bone

>Spring came
>Without pulpit flowers
>Or boiling tubs of sassafras
>A long time
>Since spring had come in a new way
>The cannons bucked like goats
>Along the edge of it
>The veins broke wide and flowered
>The corporal at Albert
>Fell into decay

In response to the bird's clarion
There came the highest qualities of gentlemen
The girls (all ladies) nursing their way through it
The towns were proud the trains the sky the liners
Staterooms wharves the skyline proud
The army proud to wear them strong as hyacinths
The surgeons were happy and proud
The wings of airplanes and proud the sheets
The pillows bedpans congressmen the subways proud
The president the frigidaire turned proud
We are proud of our girls who are over there.

> Oh, Leda, how did the swan fly in hospitals
> How from the rushes did its wings lift
> The iron mirror of the lake
> Churned to a wheel from indolence to anger
> The small black budding spring
> Pressed close between the breasts

The corporal died happy to have had
A flower nourished by his nine red yards
Of clogged intestines planted where he fell
Others were put seven hundred at a time
Under a truckload of small rock and gravel
In the way that any group
Could be disposed of without a loss to history
Beyond beauty of line squandered and wiped out
Tied still beneath gray wire wreaths with
Petits anges au ciel volez volez pour nous
Written in celluloid

> I remember them
> With Christmas trees
> With lollypops
> Eating their soup quietly
> Out of the sides of their spoons
> They made life a meal of
> Young chop suey fresh roots and tendrils
> Of peaches burning
> And of lemon ice

The corporal died knowing that if Debs
Had been president there'd be a German general
In every maiden lady's bed
Contented to masturbate the lady mules
In spare time
Talking of war not as it was to him
A burden which in honor he could not put down

    There will be more sons
    More husbands fathers
    To breed for another springtime
    To stamp for another season for hallelujah
    (Not the pruning and the sobbing of ringdoves
    In the willows soft with repining)
    Now we are stricken with peace
        We are stricken with peace
            We are stricken

                    ( 1928 )

# A VALENTINE FOR HARRY CROSBY

I offer you a heart of red eisinglass outlined in tinsel.
If you hold it up to the light you can see the sun shining through.
It is as beautiful as a goat's eye lit with anger,
It is as grave as the pines that have grown taller and taller
Lingering along the road.

Now is the year as lacy as a gown
That on the staircase runs a step or two behind
Laced with fine frost and hung with falling snow,
Soft to the ankles as a swollen stream that follows and booms down the
  shallow bed
That heels in fleeing past have spaded out: those small half moons of tender
  heels
Which rose and waned like planets in your heavens,
Young coral-nostrilled heels wading the creeks that now have broken
  through
To sniff and bleat and nibble at the edge of spring.

### THE COMPLAINT IN IT

Turn back your hair in a pompadour for the days
That have gone dwindling, that have tapered,
That have burned down to the very end.
For the days when my grandmother's hair was arrowlace

Of fern glossed red by the frost;
For the days spread like a goose's wing,
Forgotten in swivel chairs in Washington, forgotten,
In the Government Offices with a wig on, forgotten,
Forgotten, the apples rotting in the orchard,
The year left nailed in warning like a dead hawk on the barn door.

He is to be read of in history,
A gentle gentleman speaking words that shake the teeth in the head.
When the insomnia had him by the eyelids
He left his bed and walked out on the sea.
The quick little fish with their deep mouths remember

How his feet walked out on the brine of the waves.
There it is written in the cold cold hearts of them
In the cold tart blood that lies still on their bones,
How Jesus left his bed and Jesus left his women
And finely and shapely walked the salt of the sea.
The end of the tale is of Jesus like a butterfly
With his arms pinned open and his legs braided up with pain.

## THE REFRAIN

I would give you a day to go naked in.
Not this one, for it fits you badly,
And the blades of winter curved to your jaw's pumice
Whittle you to the bone.
            Other days more to your measure:
June days that pinched your weeping arm-pits, hugged the tight drums of
        your knees,
Clasped the shin drumsticks that rattled on them;
Checked April first days or double-breasted Christmases
Buttoned from gullet to ankle. But February's! with this day set in the
        middle
Like a bonfire at which to thaw your fingers.

Now is the year as lacy as a gown
Which curious winds blow up and down at will.
Hollowed for sound upon the heathen fields
The crocus quivers like a young goat's ear.
And you, what month are you, what wind that lies
As sweet as squirrel skin underneath the chin?
What time of year that sows no seeds, and reaps none,
Gives the weeded ground, the barren branch, makes way for spring
By root, by sap; draws close the February rains and bids them snuff the
        beacon of your life
To let you sleep and sleep with sleep and sleep awhile
Until a fresher season swoon between your thighs?

(1929)

# A CLOAK FOR A MAN
# WHO HAS NO HEED FOR WINTER

*to L. V.*

How often does it happen
to see fair men walk into a place where the snow has settled
with flowers fresh in their cheeks and their arms sprouting
sown thick with golden-rod and buttercup their flesh
and their eyes phlox-blue, how often do you set eye on them
dancing an avalanche with their skiis off, bringing
a bouquet of hair on the chest to lay in homage
on the remains of trees that pined away that winter?

> nor is it a light burden they carry to the high places:
> a great thirst, a wild hunger, and the iron of anger molten enough
>> within
> to brand the hide of a glacier
> a feast of hot-hearted flowers that do not bloom
> elsewhere but in their climate.

> *thou hast a thaw for winter sure as sun:*
> *and two blue beams of eyesight lashed to one*
> *to jam the breaking waters towards the spring.*
> *thou hast a burning hand that will not take*
> *gauntlet nor muff but, bare, defies the cold*
> *and smites the flanks of drifts that,*
>> *flake by flake,*
> *spume off their crust and running streams unfold.*

There was no way of knowing if it were noon in this place
unless such men, traveling fast, came into the clearing
and stood their skiis upright, like the staffs of a shepherd in the snow.
The wind changed for the better, as a woman's mind may alter,
the thaw carved the abysses out with thunder
the great trunks of the snow splintered off
struck by the color and ease of their arrival
felled as so much kindling on the flame.

*But frozen waters may sometime clap thy mouth*
*Arrows of ice be slung into the quiver.*
*Eyes drained bleak as marble of the south*
*will rattle like white dice in the river.*
> *If cold strike thee bitter, stave it off*
> *with the coarse complexion of this cloth.*

(1930)

# A GLAD DAY FOR LAURENCE VAIL

This year you gave me
The black flanks of a mule
To ripple and strain under me
And one day after another yellow as cantaloupe
Hung over my saddle like a melon-flower

The day was dark when we set out over and time was spent on face of flower too bright for ordinary weather bred to applause of bolt or thunder its petals riveted flake by flake in blue but richer. Here people and stock and vegetation breathed air not rarer but laid the nostril wide like silver rings set one upon another in. Dark was the day the flock came close for comfort asking sirup to soothe devouring shears to travel through their fleece.

But it was a glad day came after
The sun was born with a cape of fire
Came jigging stamping clapping in
It was a glad day came after

The speech that suits my ear and mouth is talk of cloth or keys or bread. A man's mind should be elsewhere. By climbing higher he pursues the sun where taste and scent and common shape have petrified have turned to glass. Quiet and pure her eye is shaped to gather landmarks herbs and flowers and mineral fists no light to set against the black advance. (But a long time I shall see the stony-footed chamois they brought in at night in a leather coat on a mule's back, like a man they had murdered, lifting him out by the chin and gazing into eyes as brown as deep as limpid death.)

But a glad day came after
The sun was born with a girdle of fire
Came stamping jigging clapping in
With his hands in his pockets and his pockets in his pants
It was a glad day came after

There is another season that comes after spring, not summer but a month who combs her hair, and braids it fast with winds and lingers late, and will not heed the elements' complaint. There is a season strips the mountains bare of twig or blade and straps with violent paths the wilderness that quivers like a carp. And rocks are stern in language and in grace as words said of them or as dance upon. Nor move not heedlessly from place to place like facile-footed men but bide their time.

There is anther season after spring when lights as white as fountains spray the north, and leaves like tar drip thickly from the bough and cast a cloak of elegance around. When odor leaps full-blown upon the stalk and music runs in hard steep flights of sound, when taste lies slow as honey in the mouth and drifts of snow lie changeless at the pass.

It was a glad day came after

Allos, when the mules come up out of the valley their old knees knuckle the skyline. There is no grip for the beasts' feet or food for their loose lips hanging other than thistles churned to fresh cream in their jaws, other than weather to flow whether to floe or mountain lake held fast. Allos, the times of year in the sireling of ewelings, in the bearing of a lamb in early darkness. Allos, under the armor which a breath might pierce, the water holds bouquets of trout and cresses. We went up to follow the spring's coming and the hard chatter of snows gone thin for water falling forever out of the mouth of sound.

It was a glad day came after
The sun was born with a hand of fire
You took me so high that the beasts faltered in sweat
We followed until twilight
The tongues of the sheep-bells calling
And your feet seeking root in the shale ahead.

(1930)

# A COMEALLYE FOR
# ROBERT CARLTON BROWN

There was one man and he was not an Irishman but he might have been one with all his lying thieving ways. Nor was he a priest but he might have been one because of his way of walking through the woods as if it were a church, murmuring, with a cross around his neck that he kept there for the shape of the thing. Gothic or Corinthian the pillars or the pine trees might have been for all he knew the difference. But if a beast were sick he could turn up its hoofs and nurse it like a mother.

> George, and will ye be my bridegroom

was the refrain in the wind and in the mosses whose species he knew in the sole of his foot. He was busy following the soft secret track of a deer running and he could not very well reply.

> And will ye be my bridegroom
> And wear a crown of glory

In stomping your foot in that impatient way, he said, you stomped out the mark of the deer or whatever it was running.

When he rolled back the sleeves of his shirt there were his arms out bare like twists of taffy. One of them he put lovingly around the soft bowed neck of the ailing cow. The lady had lost her cud, it had dropped into one of her stomachs. A cud, he said, it is made of daisy hearts and dandelions. He held a bouquet of it flowering in his hand. Her rosy tongue hung through her teeth, her noble breath lolled on this couch of flesh, her cloven feet gave battle to a thousand blades of grass.

> And will you be my bridegroom, George,
> And wear a crown of glory
> Will you take the dark for an evening cloak
> And the Pleiades for planets
> Will you dance on the turnpike with me, George

And will you shut up for half a minute, said George, until I get this cud in her mouth can't you be quiet.

He took care of the stock. He was a horse thief and a liar, it turned out. He was no good to anybody at all. Hours he wasted in making necklaces for the goats to wear to market. His fingers were as thick as dice, and just as square as. Do you think men lie still when they're dead, I said to him. Do you think men who could harpoon a whale, tan a lion, geld a stallion would ever take it lying down? I bet they stand up shouting, do you bet they're quiet? Can't you be quiet yourself, said George, until I've found one with four leaves to it?

II

When the old women went into church it was for a sight of the Bridegroom. They came along the roads and peering into the ditches, keeping their eyes and their ears cocked for a sign of him, for he was on the run. At high mass a special service was sung for him. It soared from the young boys' throats, rose high and clear against the stone and the remains of it dropped down the spine like icy drops of water.

> He is fairer than May weather and the fruit trees, they sang.
> Happy is the woman to whom he gives his hand.
>> (When he lifts up his eyes, the rivers leap with salmon.
>> He need only whistle for the waves to sound his name.)
> I have seen him cross the lake like a rainbow crossing.
> In summer he runs like a comb through the rye.
> Often have I hung my head for shame when he passed me.
> His gait is swift, his flesh is tough as leather.
> His heart is like a hawk's flight.
>> Ah-ah-ah-men!

From the altars and the chapels had the Bridegroom departed. The crosses all over the land were as empty as the loins of the Virgin. Nothing of any value had he left behind. The gold was gone from the vestry and the velvet from the wardrobe. He had stripped the braid from the bishops' dresses and cut the lace from the abbots' gowns. Somewhere, it might very well be in the bogs, he was melting down the gold of the loving cup and the silver of the tabernacle maybe.

In the church did the voices of the choirboys exhort him, but he had no time for it. He had a hand like a kick in the tail. Some of them had felt the side of it on their bottoms, not once but many's the time. No matter how loud they sung, it would do them no good now. The Bridegroom had staunched his wounds, girded up his loins, and silently gone thence.

III

## THE SONG OF THE BRIDEGROOM

I've been crying in the dark for my own land
You can know it by the way its rivers flow
Like a blindman I could find my way betwixt them
From the queer coast to the rocky jaws of Ulster
(By running my fingers over their faces would I tell them,
The northmen or the south, by the way their hearts were beating.)

I've been crying like a child for my own land
Or like a man bereaved. Let drink cascade
From mouth to heart, fall cupped in kneecap,
Cavort to temple, turn tongue to fire and breast to pulpit.
I shall die alone
Without the bride's soft arms repining
The ringdove sobbing, the marrow melting.
(By the way their color changes when I strike them drunk
Can I weed out the men of North Ireland from those of the South
And God deliver me.) Let whiskey sing requiem for us:

*Ah, what is it they have in their eye that nobody else has*
*In the curse, the kiss, the hot look on the face*
*That nobody else has. Whisper what is it or was it*
*That nobody else has and what will it ever be?*

(1930)

49

# A LANDSCAPE FOR WYN HENDERSON

Were made were not for lament for sore melodious grief were not
Were fashioned from the fox's brush tomato's heel were given
Should footfall step on mountainside would come to grief by tortuous ways
Were made for fertile valleys
So high and perilous grows despair were not for you
But wind as tasty as a seaman's cheek would stay your hand
And turn your thought to other

No cradle where to rock the head
The worms came through and riddled it
The snails strung slime birds carried off what plumes of it
To garnish rump No spinet left the flax to iron
Remains the Cave the Rock the Tree
Were not for you the avalanche but Cave turned mad with fire
For you the Rock to shape your hand for you the Tree to shelter
*I saw the snails curl up like lead I saw the worms expire.*

*The history itself began in a queer enough fashion, commenced 'dear Lydia'
written in the first of the book, and as if this in itself were not enough there was
more for your money—a photograph allowing no mistake with a feather curled
over her shoulder. 'Dear Lydia' you could say it in a hundred ways to the sight
of her and she moved not an eye nor caught a breath in her bosom. The book lay
open there with Lydia on it whenever we stepped across the room for a look at the
scorpion, and he himself swimming idly about in the glass where he survived—
someone at birth had set a face on him, an expression in the fair middle of him,
such that he wore or seemed a tall silk hat which was the rest of him as he idly
rose or struck the bottom. And for what did the woman keep him if not for her
neck when she was feeling hasty. There would he be so obliging as to draw off
her anger. A leech, said Scathewell. A scorpion, I could not call it less than. If
you'd step into the closet, said Scathewell, I could show you a scorpion for fair.
Right here in broad daylight, said I, I'll show you what a clout on the ear is.
When you've given me enough of them, said he, I can make a rosary of them.
What could be easier! But once your hand was up to strike him, then you fell to
caressing. He wore a scorpion next his skin for his love was the Virgin. A scap-
ular, he said. A scorpion, said I, it was the best I could do with it. But to see him
in pants going towards school but never to it, with books to his back and another
thought in him. To school, to school you will and thence. I respect you more, I*

*said to his back disappearing towards learning, in skirts as choirist. This dilly-*
*dallying with trousers dividing the proud carriage of, or fretting with girls I*
*will not. I'll see you wedded to the scorpion first, said I. The sacristy, said*
*Scathewell. The scorpion, said I. I would not have it other. How answer the*
*curiosity of God or stay the devil, Scathewell, if not in skirts? He swooned in the*
*confessional box and was carried out in transport. His head was light for many*
*days. They took me in to watch it on the pillow. His cheeks were hollow as cups*
*of milk. I'm making a scorpion for you, I said. A scarf, you mean, said Scathe-*
*well. I heard his voice die in the room. A scorpion, I whispered.*

My love lies here a place grown tired
    My love lay down his arms
Now here is Rock to break his heart and sand to blind his eyes with
A marmot's cry to pierce his side
To be not won by lifted foot or hair at fetlock stirring
No use to put but leap in death on whatsoever viper bird
Seek refuge from his teeth set down upon the aching throat and wait
His petals gently jaws in anguish aching
Until the blood no longer thrive
    Here grows a thistle to spur his side
Here cries a torrent to chill him
No rest will he have where he's laid him down for weapons spring beside
      him
*how can he stir when he is dead and the rain turned sharp on his weary head*
Better far let the grasses grow until they have refreshed him.

Must I be like, then let it be to shepherd met in passing
( to hear women talking amongst each other is enough and to spare to take
      their flavor from them and lavish it elsewhere
but to hear the small beasts crying at the seasons' gates or the shadow of one
      hill shouldering upon another, or to give ear to)
The music of their mouths he bore so long in solitude no words remained
( Be still, be still, in silence only can you hear)
His leather swollen as with young, with corpses left of wild mint flower or
      bones of such
His spirit lucid as a spring
Lay broad an avenue to run before while he turns this or that in search of
So opened to the elements, the young mint damsels wither
Whether for pine or cactus pale grow rarely on this stubborn land

But Cave can arch and Rock sprout fair as heaven
Cloud leaven and rise and Tree reveal its shade
(Be still, the torrent comes)
On castenetting feet the sheep complaining as they cross
The lizards skip to warmth the troating softly dies
(Be still, be still, the twig is bent the Tree is turning)

(1931)

# A STATEMENT FOR EL GRECO
# AND WILLIAM CARLOS WILLIAMS

Toledo shines out like no other city.
And Poe has risen
With his variable ways, and his jaw set at an angle.
Toledo, with no name carved to it saying: here lies.
Toledo, with the face of no man at the window.

> (With the old hairs of his beard rended in his fingers
> The past stands in the wilderness
> Lifting his staff to the heavens in wrath
> And moaning for the taste of old men in their graves
> Who have been forgotten, like these mountains of Monte Carlo,
> Dead as old shoes, with the name mountain an affront to them.
>
> The grass of them has drawn its sabers
> The stones in the heat quiver like fists shaking upon them
> Amassing a city that is taller, deeper.
>
> It is into their shadow that I would go
> With my soul quaking and my lungs made granite
> To withstand the assault of them.
>
> Not as a cloud nosing them out, nor to break the stalk of one glacial
> flower,
> Nor to sing a word that would lure them to ripening hills
> Maturing
> Their lean dry paps to udders of plenty.)

Toledo shines out like no other city
For its infernal clouds and the green of its pastures
That would bring a plague on whatever cattle or stock grazed on them,
For the unshed rain that menaces it. Toledo is the last town left standing
On the frontier, on the edge,
Before going over.

> (As in wartime, all ways led to Washington.

The streets of that city laid out for the eye of a bird,
A few hills, a few red chasms, and a wild park containing
The cages of coyotes, and buffalo in their matted capes of darky wool;
A few peacocks tailing the mild Southern air. The woods
In that part spring from under the stone roots of a statue
Who has hung her head and there grieves endlessly
For Mrs. Henry Adams, marking the sorrow that sent him
      wandering —
"Strangely unlike the prayers I prayed to you!" —
Mutely, across two generations.


There are the lawns of the White House,
A Maypole of eggs dyed primal colors, rolled by the children of Washington
While the President's Lady lifts her lorgnette and watches from the
      window.
The First Lady of the Land should stem from Southern soil,
Comprising all that grace and humor, that arch of neck and craft of bosom
For which Lord Washington unbuckled sword and scabbard,
Laid off his boots and waistcoat — that Southern elegance that chimed with
      music boxes,
Sweet corn, and indolence, that "ah," that "sah," that honey-suckled
      tongue;
Those long sweet rosy corset strings, those strings of stays lovely enough
To bind a lady's hair, carried as if a cargo of silken eiderdown transformed to
      glass;
And Washington, with his red jowls and fine calves highly turned
Reduced to dust that flies under the carriage wheels in the deep pool
Of Mount Vernon's shadow. And did he really place that firm behind
On this brocaded seat, and did that garter delicately clasp his limb?
And was this square of lace fashioned of orioles pressed to the veins, the
      pores,
The black festoons of hair that sprang in his proud nostril
From out the marrow of his British bone? )


      Toledo is the challenge.
The challenge of one man flung to the heavens,
And the heavens are the black possessed fury blowing on.
( Like Poe, with his arms crossed boldly
To conceal his shabby ruffle. )

Poe should be carved in stone facing
Four ways in Washington:
    With his cloak worn inside out and his cat beside him;
    With his arrogance, with his eyes broken,
    Facing the White House, the Treasury, the Mint, and the House of
        Representatives.
    Poe, a ham actor — Poe, a rebuke to West Point —
    Poe, a rebuke to truth, for he never spoke it —
    Accosting every passer-by with his hat extended
    Like a pauper; with his arms crossed on his tired bosom
    With his fists shaking, with his hands covering his face and the
        tears on it;
    With his smile twisted up like a ram's horn;
    There like no other Southerner —
    (Could corn meal melt in that mouth, or molasses run?
    Could any Southern sun make that heart bloom?)

As in wartime, they all turned to Washington; Poe, Whitman, asking a
    place to keep soul and body together
In the Government offices — in the Customs — "I should be glad," wrote Poe,
    "if you would take an opportunity
Of saying to Mr. Rob Tyler that if he can look over matters
And get me the inspectorship I will join the Washingtonians forthwith."

    ("Don't say a word about the cloak turned inside out
    Or other peccadilloes of that nature.")

"I think it would be a feather in Mr. Tyler's cap to save from the perils of
    Mint Julep...
A young man of whom all the world thinks so well and who thinks
remarkably well of himself!"

    Poe, you have disarmed me. Your courage has taken my strength
        from me.
    Poe, you have broken me.
    There is no spirit left to me, because of you.

Don't say a word about the Mint Juleps,
Don't say a word about being sick on the floor.
Please say I'm sorry about the Don's mustaches,

The port wine, the coffee, and the barbershop's score.
Don't let them know my wife has hemorrhages —
She strained her throat at singing was what I said —
Don't say a word about the house being buggy.
Please apologize for all the silly things I said.

Washington, you would have stepped the minuet gustily with any woman;
Your head in its wig would have swooned for any mouth.
Toledo has made all other cities barren.
Toledo has made the Cross burgeon and bloom.

It is set there among all the pictures of men's faces
The Crucifixion, with the clouds like boulders
Knuckling Christ's head. Had you not spoken
These things would not have been so: not the root dug white and clear
With the smell of the earth on it,
But a slow fire in the underbrush and no shadow of respite cast
Upon the flame that has taken my timber as fuel.

( You have laid waste the pastures that stretch beyond me
And I would return to excavations exhorting you
To speak of what lies in our stones:

Toledo, from the brush of a dead man;
Forbears, from the speech of a living. )

( 1931 )

# A WATERFRONT FOR
# ALLAN ROSS MACDOUGALL

There are two sides to it:
the port at the quay holding sweet hay and fodder
for the prows and the flanks in the water leaping
wilder and shyer than foals at the halter.

Or the beach pure as linen with ornaments brought there
by night on the tide and set down for the feasting:
sea-urchins and molluscs and long loving octopus arms
clasped blushing in death as they wither.

Such is the sea and the coast there
dry as a skull and the foliage
needled and thorned and fruitless
and the white sand borne by the mistral
fir by fir to the dancing.

### THE TRAGEDY

Knowing that the springs have swung low year after year for sailors sleep-
ing but once in the room and passing, knowing that the heart strikes there
in solitude mighty as a ship's black shuddering heart:

Maxim I'm sending you this few lines to ask you to write Maxim just to say
what were they the reasons for why you didn't come back Sunday Maxim
why was it you went to the trouble you did to tell me all the things you did
Maxim you might as well know I don't think you're much of a man by this
time you can be sure of that. My God Maxim I was the poor fool I'll say to
believe what you said I should have looked out it's about time now I got my-
self caught. You can take the credit too for the way I cry all the time Maxim I
won't keep it from you any longer that I love you and I'll always love you like
the song says for always Maxim I'll love the baby the dear little thing that's
coming you can be sure I'll do everything like a mother Maxim to bring him
up right I'll give him a good home and the best of everything Maxim as for
my life it's finished unless you would do what you promised to didn't you
Maxim. If you would do that you won't be sorry. I'll make things nice for
you I'll go on the street if that would please you Maxim I've got a place cook-
ing for a family until I'm 21 Maxim when I can get into a house and be no
better than a prostitute to bring up the dear little boy. Now Maxim if you

want to answer about the little baby that's coming like a father would here's my address of one who will always be crying for her Maxim until he does what he said he would and then we'll have a nice life together like I wrote.

Knowing the whisper and hush of vessels moored and unsaddled and their bridles laid aside for the night.

> There are two sides to it:
> the storming and the fair weather
> and the sea outspoken as a man speaks
> or its peace held fawning
> quiet and sly like a woman
> There are the green waters folded and unfolded
> and the sea stamping at night
> offering love like a negress dancing.

> Scotland, it might be, without the shadow or the wet cheeks
> of the highlands but the fog with a match to it
> the heather and the gorse ablaze there
> the lakes of the country ignited.

## THE COMEDY

St Raphael and towns to eastward stand (gentlemen gentlemen hasten past this shore) in frescoes baked upon the peeling land, fancy as valentines in summer would outdo (gentlemen money has a hollow ring) the pink of dawn and rival southern blue (gentlemen give me this instead) the toiling ocean bears with their pretense (gentlemen gentlemen drown your wavy hair) save, when the seasons change, its eloquence hurls wild on Agay and such flippant places (build your courage blast by blast) whose walls are painted like unworthy faces. (Gentlemen learn ignorance like a book) let those who cherish a proud and fervent heart (gentlemen tear the hair upon your chests) turn westward on the wedded roads that part at Frejus (gentlemen gentlemen flattery withers fast) and with ribboned espadrilles on follow the long white lonely sands (gentlemen speak of what you know) to Toulon, stopping wherever the nets are out and giving (gentlemen what have you to give?) hand to the seamen, dine where Meille is living (crack the lobsters claw by shell) the maquis makes a mattress white as ether here (gentlemen gentlemen put your words away.)

(1931)

58

# FUNERAL IN HUNGARY

Rakob is dead, what is left of him travels
The ruts and the road puddles granite with frost.
He is dead and his Sunday suit on him, and the look of the dead
Like a wreath on his mouth for a while.

Six white oxen with black ribbons entwined
In their horns draw his hearse. He is lighter than pigroot,
Not so heavy as dung to them. Their collars are timber,
Their mouths slobber sweet with the morning.

Around his corpse roam the gypsy musicians
Singing wild high nostalgic, their gut strings bewailing
That Rakob is dead. Behind come the cattle
Yoked two by two, their tails hanging clean as silk tassels,
The weight moving slow as a heart's beat from split hoof to split hoof.

Behind, drawn by four piebald oxen, the family of Rakob
Wears clothes that are festive, the horns of the oxen
Are twisted with flowers. The music that stamps on foot by their wheels
Is foreign to grief; the jigs and the reels of the country dances
Danced with the flute and accordion playing.

Rakob wrote down the way these things should be,
Leaving his cattle and lands, his fortune and words
Set down in his last will and testament, saying:
"My cattle were my peaceful friends. Let them follow close to me when I go
          towards the grave.
Because of their innocence I have taken them into my heart
As if they were little children who came to me.
None of my people feel for them the gratitude they have earned
So I have put aside for them a portion of my wealth that they may die in
          peace,
Not of abuse, while laboring in the fields as they have always done.
I bid my relatives to follow me with music playing, wearing
Their dance dresses and colored waistcoats. My death will bring them ease
And so they must rejoice. I ask them not to allow the temptations of the city

To seduce them. Only a knowledge of the seasons can bring dignity to man.
But let an orchestra of gypsies wander beside me grieving
Who have cause to grieve now that their horses may no longer
Roam at night grazing in my pastures, now that they may no longer in the
    darkness
Gather my pine brush and light fires unmolested underneath my trees."

( 1 9 3 5 )

# A COMPLAINT FOR MARY AND MARCEL

*I believe in the
scenic railways
that have not
run yet because
the scaffolding
is still unsafe
and in the
buildings they
have not had
time to finish
I believe this
year and this
time of the
year there is
never the time
to finish only
the time left to
begin again.*

*If it is wiser
to say too
little than
too much there
being less to
take back in
anguish later
then it is
easier to say
too much for it
leaves that
much less to
carry about in
the veins
seeking to say
it or not to
say it or not to
remember to*

You did not come to the Paris
    exposition of 1937 on the
    opening night when I
    asked you.
You did not see the fountains fresh
    as lilacs spraying along the
    river in the dark
Or the fans they had bought for the
    occasion made of blue lace and
    used instead of illumination.
You did not wait behind the scenes
    in the wings for the actors to
    come and the curtain to rise
Or the cues to be given. You were
    not there when the searchlights
    poured the milk of avalanches
Into the obliterated alley of the
    Seine.

Where you were you could not hear
    the roman candles breaking the
    way glass breaks under a fist
Or say with a thousand other people
    who were there "Ah-h-h-h"
    with the voice of one person
Awed when the tour Eiffel was
    transformed to burning wire,
    nor could you see
The fireworks climb like larks in
    spring to those explosions of
    indecipherable mystery
That liberate metal or song more valuable
    than money is. The savagery
Of serpents and birds imported from
    Japan pursued their own
    incalculable wealth
In emeralds, diamonds, rubies, and

*say it or to*
*forget it is not*
*things like this*
*that can be*
*said.*

topaz, writhing and spiraling
    through the firmament,
Crashing in thirst and frenzy through
    the tropic underbrush that
    leafed in conflagrated satin
Trunked in seething palm and cocoa hair
    the sky's wild blistering jungle.

*You did not*
*visit the Belgian*
*or the Russian*
*or the Italian*
*or the German*
*pavilions or ride*
*up in the lift with*
*the smell of roses*
*thick as smoke*
*but sweeter in*
*your eyes. You*
*were expecting*
*Man Ray or*
*Nancy Perry or*
*Dali or Brancusi*
*to come and sit in*
*the garden with the*
*tiger lilies with you.*

You had people to dinner. You could
    not come. You did not see the
    small thick hooded candles
They set out like gondolas on the
    current, drifting in slow
    flickering formation like folded
    gulls
With hearts ignited moving a-light
    upon the river's or the tide's
    declining.
They were extinguished one by one
    by breath or wind or by their
    own defatigation
( As the complaints I set out lighted
    in the dark for you expire in
    their passage
Because of the long way through
    silence they must go. )

## THE STORY I WANTED TO TELL YOU

Well, when I got up to the top of the German pavilion I thought I'd die laughing, for there was a man I'd seen dead at least twice in his life. He was wearing a waiter's white jacket, the kind he'd worn when he was an Austrian barman and he was carrying the steins of beer people had ordered, three in each hand by the handles. There was just one difference in him: he'd broken his leg at the ankle ski-jumping since I'd seen him last and he was limping. It was so hot there was a string of priceless beads bound to his forehead; he was so pale that when I gave him the rose the color from its petals was reflected an instant on his face. He put down the steins of beer on the stone rail instead of on the tables and he said My God you look awful, and I said Hubert you look simply terrible. We'd been waiting two years to say things to each other and these were the words that came the quickest. The fireworks had begun outside like war on the river, giving the people a taste of what they wanted and the perfect aspect of the night a lust to civilize it for consumption, and Hubert and I did not sit down and did not stand up but watched the foam perish on the beer he had forgotten. What month did you die in, Hubert, I said, and he said, It must have been May. You know you look very badly, he said. You look very thin. It was that afternoon we were going up too late in the year and the side of the Grossglockner gave up what snow was left. Over the thunder of the tons of it falling I could still hear his voice like the cry of a marten, the last breaths he drew the plucked strings of a harp humming still. There was no more life in his face then than now except for the eyes bleached golden as his hair and sightless as a cameo's. The whole south side avalanched that month, he said, it must have been in May. However it was, I said, you were alive and kicking next October. We went to Vienna for the newborn wine, we were in at the birth, we danced ourselves sick. I began laughing again, looking at Hubert and laughing until my cheeks ached from laughing out loud and I said I remember the place they buried you was standing wide open Christmas eve in the churchyard. I went there with a little tree for you with the candles lighted on it and silk ribbons tied in its branches. I fooled them, said Hubert, and I said, Hubert your English is beautiful and your French is music and your German makes the edelweiss grow colder sharper purer in my heart.

Well, the upshot of it all was that he broke his shoulder skiing ahead of me on the Fleck Alp. Blood poisoning set in right away and in twenty-four hours he was dead to the world. You paid your debt to nature once too often, Hubert my love, I said, you crossed the Stygian ferry without me, you shuffled off this mortal coil. You went out like the snuff of a candle, passed in your chips, you launched into eternity without my arm in your arm. Hubert held up his hand against the convulsions of the aerial display and I could count the bones in it and see the illuminations shining through it as if through mist and he said Look the blood is gone from it, not flowed away put parched the way a spring will dry.

When they let you into the room at the hospital that night it was all over, Hubert said. I'd died half an hour before. Listen, Hubert, I said, I didn't take a drink all day that day so as to be able to walk straight past the other beds to you. You kneeled down but you didn't cry, Hubert said, but anyway I kept all the things you said to me. I said them out loud to myself all night and all during the funeral service the priest was saying for me laying me away in death. What was it I said to you, I asked him, and Hubert answered: Whenever they put a shovelful of earth slap down on my face I kept saying what you'd said faster and faster until they got me down for good and choked me with it. If you want any beer you can damned well get up and get it yourselves, Hubert said, for the people had risen from the tables on the roof-garden of the German pavilion whether to see the fireworks better or to ask for drink. I've been trying to put weight on all spring, said Hubert. We were standing so close together that there was no need to move or to embrace each other. After one has burned to death, he said, putting out his thin hands where I could see them, it is impossible to keep the flesh on one's bones.

And then the whole truth of the thing came out and everything else I knew about him might have been something somebody made up. It seems that after he died in the hospital that winter or that May in the Alps then nothing would do but he must get a job on an airship and he wouldn't hear of anything else and he'd get it willy-nilly. He'd get it no matter what, he said, and come what may. And listening to him telling me I suddenly knew and pushed his hand aside in fright and I went running out through the people with my high heels turning sideways in panic with every step I ran. I went crying in terror down the flights of stairs with the heat of the furnace laying waste behind me, the fire after me in pursuit like a crowd of people running fast, some roaring, some whispering through roasted lips, the flames after me relentlessly in truth with the split and the rip of their conflagration pouring in torrents of rushing fire down the cascade of flight to lower flight. At the entrance door below I could not pass, for the skeleton stood there waiting. The rose I had given him was in his fingers still, the petals charred and the leaves ash-white and ready to dissolve in dust. After much difficulty I finally succeeded, he said, in getting a place as steward on the Hindenburg. The trip over the sea was beautiful. I wish you had been there.

YOUR LOVE SONG

Here or in any public place you may begin to sing
The violent serenade that rises with the tide of drink's
Green icy rising that once plunged in thaws to flesh
And melts the veins to music, turns your tongue
To harp or cello weeping notes of love. Drinking and talking fast

You will begin the overture to invocation lovely as a horn's clear
    winding
And unloose the garments of your eloquence to lay them down before
    him.
I have heard you sing

sweet as a nightingale at the articulation of that grotesque hymn which lies
in necks of bottles springing for escape from silence. The pitiless eye on you
over the unlifted glass, you, peacock-headed, do burst into song and,
sheeny-throated, marvelously sing such words of beauty that his nights and
days swoon with delight, slumber in glamour, leap like winds at morning
straight into the sun. This symphony that whirls and hurls venom through
anguish into purity transforms shit, whore, patroness, bitch, and parasite to
declaration tender enough for children's ears to hear. You do exalt him limb
by limb to power richer than any man's, bedeck his brows with flowers the
thorns are torn from by your hand, endow his eye with sight that sheds its
spears in every woman's flesh, inspire his blood until his foot does beckon to
the dance, steps the implacable jig your voice plays hotly, intemperately,
and tireless as lovers.

    The sweet high declaration that it has
    Impugns the air unlike the sound of what
    Is recognized as it: ( as if the speech of it
    Could lie at rest upon the tongue
    As soft as arms around the neck, or weave
    From mouth to ear or mouth to mouth as kisses weave. )
    It may be sung without rehearsal any night
    At bars or café tables; it may suddenly rise
    The way a statue in the falling dark
    Discards its marble and its classic eyes.

(1937)

# A COMMUNICATION TO NANCY CUNARD

These are not words set down for the rejected
Nor for outcasts cast by the mind's pity
Beyond the aid of lip or hand or from the speech
Of fires lighted in the wilderness by lost men
Reaching in fright and passion to each other.
This is not for the abandoned to hear.

It begins in the dark on a boxcar floor, the groaning timber
Stretched from bolt to bolt above the freight-train wheels
That grind and cry aloud like hounds upon the trail, the breathing weaving
Unseen within the dark from mouth to nostril, nostril to speaking mouth.
This is the theme of it, stated by one girl in a boxcar saying:
"Christ, what they pay you don't keep body and soul together."
"Where was you working?" "Working in a mill town."
The other girl in the corner saying: "Working the men when we could get
    them."
"Christ, what they pay you," wove the sound of breathing, "don't keep
    shoes on your feet.
Don't feed you. That's why we're shoving on."

( This is not for Virginia Price or Ruby Bates, the white girls dressed like
boys to go; not for Ozie Powell, six years in a cell playing the little harp he
played tap-dancing on the boxcar boards; not for Olen Montgomery, the
blind boy traveling toward Memphis that night, hopping a ride to find a
doctor who could cure his eyes; not for Eugene Williams or Charlie Weems,
not for Willie Robertson nor for Leroy and Andy Wright, thirteen years old
the time in March they took him off the train in Paint Rock, Alabama; this is
not for Clarence Norris or Haywood Patterson, sentenced three times to
die. )

This is for the sheriff with a gold lodge pin
And for the jury venireman who said: "Now, mos' folk don't go on
And think things out. The Bible never speaks
Of sexual intercourses. It jus' says a man knows a woman.
So after Cain killed Abel he went off and knew a woman
In the land of Nod. But the Bible tells as how
There couldn't be no human folk there then.

Now, jus' put two and two together. Cain had offspring
In the land of Nod so he musta had him a female baboon
Or chimpanzee or somethin' like it.
And that's how the nigger race begun."

This is for the Sunday-school teacher with the tobacco plug
Who addressed the jury, the juice splattering on the wall,
Pleading: "Whether in overalls or furs a woman is protected by the Alabama
    law
Against the vilest crime the human species knows. Now, even dogs choose
    their mates,
But these nine boys are lower than the birds of the air,
Lower than the fish in the sea, lower than the beasts of the fields.
There is a law reaching down from the mountaintops to the swamps and
    caves —
It's the wisdom of the ages, there to protect the sacred parts of the female
    species
Without them having to buckle around their middles
Six-shooters or some other method of defense."

This is set down for the others: people who go and come,
Open a door and pass through it, walk in the streets
With the shops lit, loitering, lingering, gazing.
This is for two men riding, Deputy Sheriff Sandlin, Deputy Sheriff
    Blacock,
With Ozie Powell, handcuffed. Twelve miles out of Cullman
They shot him through the head.


THE TESTIMONY


*Haywood Patterson:*                      *Victoria Price:*
"So here goes an I shell try
Faitfully an I possibly can
Reference to myself in particularly              "I
And concerning the other boys               cain't
    personal pride                       remember."
And life time upto now.
You must be patiene with me
    and remember


6 7

Most of my English is not of
  much interest
And that I am continually
Stopping and searching for the
  word."

"I
cain't
remember."

So here goes and I shall try faithfully as possible to tell you as I understand if not mistaken that Olen Montgomery, who was part blind then, kept saying because of the dark there was inside the boxcar and outside it: "It sure don't seem to me we're getting anywheres. It sure don't seem like it to me." I and my three comrades whom were with me, namely Roy Wright and his brother Andy and Eugene Williams, and about my character I have always been a good natural sort of boy, but as far as I am personally concerned about those pictures of me in the papers, why they are more or less undoubtedly not having the full likeness of me for I am a sight better-looking than those pictures make me out. Why all my life I spent in and around working for Jews in their stores and so on and I have quite a few Jew friends whom can and always have gave me a good reputation as having regards for those whom have regards for me. The depression ran me away from home, I was off on my way to try my very best to find some work some elsewhere but misfortune befalled me without a moving cause. For it is events and misfortune which happens to people and how some must whom are less fortunate have their lives taken from them and how people die in chair for what they do not do.

### THE SPIRITUAL FOR NINE VOICES

I went last night to a turkey feast (Oh, God, don't fail your children
  now!)
My people were sitting there the way they'll sit in heaven
With their wings spread out and their hearts all singing
Their mouths full of food and the table set with glass
(Oh, God, don't fail your children now!)
There were poor men sitting with their fingers dripping honey
All the ugly sisters were fair. I saw my brother who never had a penny
With a silk shirt on and a pair of golden braces
And gems strewn through his hair.

(Were you looking, Father, when the sheriffs came in?
Was your face turned towards us when they had their say?)

68

There was baked sweet potato and fried corn pone
There was eating galore, there was plenty in the horn.

(Were you there when Victoria Price took the stand?
Did you see the state attorney with her drawers in his hand?
Did you hear him asking for me to burn?)

There were oysters cooked in amplitude
There was sauce in every mouth.
There was ham done slow in spice and clove
And chicken enough for the young and the old.

(Was it you stilled the waters on horse-swapping day
When the mob came to the jail? Was it you come out in a long tail coat
Come dancing high with the word in your mouth?)

I saw my sister who never had a cent
Come shaking and shuffling between the seats.
Her hair was straight and her nails were pointed
Her breasts were high and her legs double-jointed.

(Oh, God, don't fail your children now!)

THE SENTENCE

Hear how it goes, the wheels of it traveling fast on the rails
    The boxcars, the gondolas running drunk through the night.
Hear the long high wail as it flashes through stations unlit
    Past signals ungiven, running wild through a country
A time when sleepers rouse in their beds and listen
    And cannot sleep again.
Hear it passing in no direction, to no destination
Carrying people caught in the boxcars, trapped on the coupled chert cars
(Hear the rattle of gravel as it rides whistling through the day and night.)
Not the old or the young on it, nor people with any difference in their color
    or shape,
Not girls or men, Negroes or white, but people with this in common:
People that no one had use for, had nothing to give to, no place to offer
But the cars of a freight train careening through Paint Rock,
    through Memphis,

Through town after town without halting.
The loose hands hang down, and swing with the swing of the train in
    the darkness,
Holding nothing but poverty, syphilis white as a handful of dust,
    taking nothing as baggage
But the sound of the harp Ozie Powell is playing or the voice of
    Montgomery
Half-blind in oblivion saying: "It sure don't seem to me like we're
    getting anywheres.
It don't seem to me like we're getting anywheres at all."

(1937)

# ANGELS FOR DJUNA BARNES

Persuaded you walk alone, alone walk naked, what veins of Ireland
What America, gold, rollinghipped, what tightlipped pioneering, what
    deepbreasted orient
In your transversal of sentiment: its failing sands
Its rutted road, its mackerel way macadamized; the ancient paved
*Piazzas* of the firmament where pigeons continuous as angels
Sweep the winds moaning and lividly scar with lime the worthless stone
Of architecture. Alone mount the primitive hills
Crown them with appletrees in full bruised waxy flower, alone
Stand gazing drunkwise into vastation where vast rivers mutely
In choral silence falter in their accustomed beds and worship.

(“The secret is fresher than rainbows, stabler than mountains,
Agreeing with flowers, with tides and the rising and setting of
    autumnal stars.”)*

Persuaded you do not walk, nor alone advance nor embrace naked
But stepless go, white breast to wingtip, shoulder to lip, pinions spread
    cavernous
For the celestial flight described as motion's illumination, taking the
    circular
The oblique and the straight as simultaneous direction, mate with
Velocity as angels wed in keeping with the threefold will
Unbroken as a colt's heart on the plains in wind; the act of angels soaring
Not motion but contact achieved in varying altitudes with varying degrees
    of space;
So you arise, torn like a woman but assume the shape
Of air. Djuna, the love you dress in black for and the love I bear are decked
    alike
In convicts' bracelets that link wrist to wrist; were made immediately
Composed like angels in imperfect sanctity; were made in grace
In the Empyrean sky, part action, part potentiality.

The orchid you first gave me has not died
But in a tracery of itself survives as ghosts are said to live

* Emerson's “Representative Men.”

In torment of the fear of death, unable to remember
They have died. ( Aquinas' devotion asked if Christ were not
       hermaphrodite
And if the pious at resurrection would arise with excrement
Still in them; and if the angel Gabriel appeared to Her in light
As serpent, dove, or man, or girl; if during conception
Mary remained seated or if She reclined, and if reclining
Did Christ lie with Her or remain erect; if angels know things clearer in the
       morning or
What number of angels can dance on the point of a fine needle
Without impinging on one another; if angels pass from one extreme
To the next without going through the middle; whether the angel Gabriel's
       linen
Were clean or foul, and if the book She read upon his coming
Were not the Book of Sentences. ) Persuaded you do not know
But seek and strike your own face for another's, forget your dream
While dreaming, do not wake nor sleep but halted in wild motion
Lie, quiver, stand, are held to the ear for roar of music like a shell held
Or like a statue found beneath the sand, still limbed, still whole, still marble
The mouth with terra cotta, eyes with salt weeping for mutilation.

Djuna, to treat of angels must one give
Name to their substance, offices, and grace;
Conceive they move towards death or never live
Or are contained in or contain all space?
An angel's constant motion is not spent
Nor ebbs to quiet, nor declines in tread:
Convoked again in wind's or tide's ascent
Describes the sequence of the fruitful dead.
The throat to angels is the horn of love
Hollowed by singing, clasped by women's hands
Sex unicorned, winged simply as the dove
Who sunwards crosses heaven's shifting sands.
       Maidened by constant springtime, angels refluent go
       Towards youth, not age, and purer shyer grow.

(1937)

# WORLD TOUR

*for my daughter, Sharon*

Take determination, take it apart; stamp out the music from its means,
Meet the violently fixed eyes of its enacted ends, split
Not the origins but the performances of war and peace and in
Their sundered dramas watch the actors fail, fumble their lines,
The curtain quiver to rise and then expire; take gray-leafed mimosa,
Palm, marigold, planted as regular as prison stripes along the new
Italian roads laid to conduct the world's tour of the curious and idle through
Poverty; take them and break their stems for sap, and as they wither hear
It whispered: "We are committed not to fade whatever the season;
Like iron vegetation, neither to wilt or shed petal so no eye reads
Between our leaves the lices' determination in children's hair, the
Scleritis flung into their eyes like red hot sand." This open air
You take within your substance then expel, isolates the open, jaunty, tragic,
Lordly, free; tainted by method, pock-marked with spit, employed by
          Franco in soliciting
Tourists this summer to come visit, relax in; see the trapped speechless air
Of Negroes and the mob already at the door, or that the old and nameless
Jews, scientists or tradesmen too obscure for ransom wear. Take ransom,
Take it: a frantic accumulation of grief, protest, and fury paid
Year after gullible year before the mutilated corpse of youth is found,
Rain-sodden, its betrayed mouth set, dead at the very moment
The currency was passed and rotting in the underbrush of home.

          ( You know, I had the funniest dream last night,
          She said when she came home from school.
          I was standing in the chapel just like every day
          And all the other kids were there, of course,
          And then this man, you know, a kind of short thin man,
          Came in and took the middle of the floor
          As if he was going to make a speech or something.
          But before he got a word out, I don't know how it was,
          The whole top of his head started to burn.
          Oh, I forgot to say that all the time
          He had his hand up in, you know, like the fascist salute
          And his other hand was held up shaking in a clenched fist all the time.
          Well, after his head caught on fire, he kept on burning,

His hair, and face, and neck, and everything straight down
And nobody did anything or said a word. It was cuckoo.
But just before his shoes burned he said: "Vive
La Patrie!" I don't know what said it, I mean,
Whether it was his shoes said it or what, but
Anyway he said: "Vive la Patrie!" with a funny accent
Like a foreigner trying to speak French, and in my dream
I did the dumbest thing. I fell down on my knees
In front of all the other kids and started praying.)

Come here, come in with me and let follow
Those faces which pursue you:
The sick, wild, reticent, at bay,
Who do not crowd but quietly heel
And do not want but take the glass to drink
And cannot, but let spill, let fall,
Let dribble down their chins, let go
Pride's remnants, massacred but quick still,
Clotted, jugulated veins, conduits
In bleeding fragments, valves to gasp
Flapping from the air's white strangling net
Down shirt front to floor and there not stop
Their dying. Come in and say it. Let
The gaunt musicians begin, let the outcast, the hungry, condemned,
Tied ankle to ankle and coupled,
Jerk the marathon dance, stumble drunk
To the music, but sober, swoop low to the boards
At the last, but change partners and hands for the lynching.

(1938)

74

# AMERICAN CITIZEN

## COLORADO 1943

Here stand the mountains of this state—
They speak his name.
They give it substance beyond accident.
The red rock of the skeleton they share
Is bared by January thaw, ancient, unbroken, violent,
Fierce as a long-dead Indian's hand clenched still—
But weaponless—beneath the temporary snow.
All mountains where
The fir trees mount, black-hoofed, erect, swiftly as deer,
Gait silent as a savage's, pronounce his name—
The first name and the last—signal it where
Pine needles fall soundless as spangles from a lady's dress
His fingers touch the throat of; record it silently
In ski track, the motion of a weighted branch, announce
That he climbed fast, paused here and there,
Beat the cold from his hands, roared out with laughter
At a bear's shuffle across the snow's parquet
Or the wild skid of a hare.

This is a hard state. No quarter is given.
The soil at this height in this month of the year
Must be blasted by dynamite for an interring.
This is a hard year. There are no favors to ask of it,
No use to cry at the door of it: "Let other men go!
He has done what the men of Europe have done,
Done it quietly as the drawing of breath, done it waltzing and cursing,
Done it in chain gangs, done it laughing out loud,
Done it crying when the cold of the season exacted
That homage be paid it, as tears are, from the eyes."
I cannot beat with my fists at this year's austerity,
Saying: "Let other hearts break this time, not his.
His was broken on glaciers, broken in pastures, broken
On rock peaks horned sharp as antlers
Where he could no longer speak the name of home."

This is a hard time. Let him dance to the end
To the music of it. He is a young man. It is only the old
And the empty-hearted who sit the last waltz out
While the music plays.

## THE INVITATION IN IT

Carson, turn your coat collar up, throw the cigarette from your hand
And dance with me. The mazurka of women is easy to learn.
It is danced by the young, the high-heeled, and the doll-faced
Who swing on the bar stools, their soft drinks before them.
The polka of war brides is easy to follow. They dance down the streets
With their legs bare, their coats hanging open. In their pockets
Are letters written from home to be opened
Not to be read, but ripped wide by the fingernail (varnished
The color of blood), to be shaken for the check or the money order,
The dollar bill folded. These are the honeymooners
In one-room shacks, in overnight cabins, in trailer camps, dancing
The *pas seul* in shoes that strap fast at the ankle, talking
G.I. talk as if they had learned it not this year,
Not here, but months at the breast, years learning to spell still.
"Sweating out three weeks of maneuvers, or sweating the week-end pass,
Or sweating him out night after night," they'll say, sweet-tongued as
        thrushes.
"Say, who's fighting this war, the M.P.'s or our husbands?" they'll ask
As they swing on the bar stools. Their voices may say:
"Up on Kiska last year, he lost eighty bucks in a crap game
And twelve playing cards, two weeks before Christmas,"
While the music plays on for the dancers; or say:
"This is my ring. How do you like it? We didn't have diamonds
Put in this year. We can get them cheaper back home.
We were going to have something engraved inside. We wanted 'forever'
Engraved, but we didn't have time yet," or saying:
"The night I had fever he wanted to go over the hill,"
But where is the hill that is high enough, wild enough, lost enough
Leading away? (Carson, dance with me.) This is the waltz
Of the wives whose men are in khaki. Their faces are painted
As flawless as children's, their hearts each the flame of a candle
That his breath can extinguish at will.

7 6

# THE WALTZ TUNE IN IT

Drink is the strange, sweet, winding road
Which leads men into strangers' arms, women to men's,
Taps swifter than alcoholic pulse the dancing feet.
Here in the Colorado bar the Danube's blue streamed,
Reeled the Vienna woods in springtime, tapped the one, two, three,
Faster and faster spun the web, and the skirt that was short
Billowed soft and wide in its embrace of khaki no longer
But the slim legs, waltzing and swooning as they wove, of the uniformed
    Hussar.
There might be the music of gophers playing,
The intricate, delicate step in the road's dust; here
The flat-pawed passage of beavers over the Colorado rock —
Except it is January, and the snow is falling.
It is the time of year
For one man in khaki to set the Hussar aside,
To start down a wiped-out road on the mountain, leaving camp on foot,
And make it on foot through the snow from Pando to Redcliff,
Slog on from Redcliff to Minturn, speaking
His name in violence through his teeth to the cold.

"This is my name," he will say. "I have seen it on roll calls before,
On the lists of those wanted. It was called on the deck
Of one ship in the harbor of Marseille, and I answered 'present.'
But that day it was only the Spaniards who went, led back to shore
With the sad wild eyes of their women on them. That day it was only the
    men
Returned to their country for execution, while their women and children
    sailed.
Ours is a bitter history," he will say, "for we are a generation that has lived as
    traitors live,
Not in the fear of death, but in the fear of being led across our own frontiers
Again. This is my name," he will say in tight-lipped fury to the wind and the
    snow.
"You cannot take it from me. I have seen it on rosters of other camps than
    this,
Camps where men's bones in internment were, like their names, broken
    and scattered

And bleached like driftwood, and like driftwood were rejected even by the
    tide.
This is not Colorado, this is not the West, this is not January even.
I have left not an army camp tonight, but my own soil. Let Pando
Be Austria then, and I still Austrian. Here the mountains stand similarly
    high,
But they are rugged. The Austrian mountains are Mozart's — modest and
    tender and inexpressibly starred with light.
I leave them, monuments erected to my country, not leaving Redcliff
To slog on to Minturn, but crossing from Austria by the Brenner,
Taking the high frontier." The snow was thick underfoot that night
And the wind cold. It was a long way to come to a barroom,
And this was the game of history played with his footsteps through the
    dark:
"I am not an American soldier walking through Colorado canyons
Towards a glass of Scotch and the tune I want in the jukebox, and the
    woman I want in my arms.
I am one of an army of lost men who follow a point of the compass
In common. We will not be single, undetermined men walking alone again
Until our feet are breaking through the snows of home."

He will say: "I crossed my own mountains into others because it was asked
    of me,
Asked as inaudibly as a finger laid on the lips for silence, but to which the
    blood
Gave answer as if it were asked louder and clearer than the iron clamor
Of a tocsin's bell." So he waltzes the waltz
From Pando to Redcliff, Redcliff to Minturn, Minturn to Eagle, as he reeled
    it once
Before them in Europe, not outcast this time, not dissenter, not Hussar
Even, but soldier in khaki and sheepskin, stamping his history from Eagle
    to Glenwood
With the snow packed white to his knees.

This is the month to remember, this the state,
Because of one man's feet in the waltz, his arm at the waist,
His nickels keeping the jukebox lit
While other men's voices on the bakelite disks
Shook the words of grief like dice in the room.
This is the loud, fast tune we stamped out that night

To silence the whimper; this the small glass taken straight
For the swooning steps and the tears. The wrists
Were bound fast at the back, the bowed neck was shaved
The month that he walked all night through the snow.
There was nothing
But the eyes glazed bright in the waltz now that the time
For the taste of the last cigarette on his lips, for the last glass of brandy,
Now that the hour was set for the execution, for the last, quick beat of his
    shoes on the boards
And the leave-taking was there.

Here there should be an accordion playing, a harmonica trebling the quick,
    sweet notes;
There should be red-throated valleys calling the music of rapids and trout
    flesh —
Except it is January. It is the season
For one man to stamp the snow from his feet, ask for Scotch,
Light the lights in the jukebox; for the hard-jawed, hard-knuckled women
To soften as the music begins, and the trays with the drinks on them
To tip sideways in their hands.

## THEY ARE OVERSEAS

Carson, the days are long this year. The feet are not dancing. There are the
    letters that come
Or do not come. I look into your pale, young face and your lips move,
And, as if this were a mirror I look into, the words they shape in silence are
    the same.
They say: "I do not believe that young men die by violence. I do not believe
That men who have waltzed to music, ordered Scotch at a bar,
Outwitted snow, wind, rain, survived the mountain heights — "
They say: "I have whispered his name in sleep to him.
I carry it now like a bell's tongue in my heart."

Carson, the days are long this year. Our dreams are interchangeable,
Your dreams with mine and mine with yours, mingling as gracefully as do
    all women's dreams in war.
Those who mourn say there is still the alphabet of sorcery to learn

In solace. ( Shall we go together, look for the number in the street, climb the
     shabby stairs
To the tables, to the cups set for tea on the checkered cloth? Shall we
Move quietly, faceless as ghosts, without identity through the half-lit room,
Sit down to wait for the woman in the flowered dress to come? Shall we
Bare our palms to her under the seer's light, watch her play out

The cards before us, hear the tea leaves read, give ear to the words spoken
Over fire, respect the vision conjured in the crystal ball?)
*Women in bereavement turn to this. They lie unsleeping, toss in the darkness,*
*Empty-armed, see the wound in his flesh, count the hours of agony*
*Before he died. Hear, night after night, his last cry drawn from the scabbard of*
     *the naked throat,*
*Striking each time deeper and more fatally. They say*
*There is still the alphabet of sorcery to learn in solace, as slowly, painfully,*
*As hungrily as the blind learn Braille.*

Carson, the days are long this year. They break the heart. ( Shall we
Heed sorcery's seduction now, wait for the woman in the flowered dress to
     come
To the table, empty the cups of tea so that the alphabet of leaves remains?
Shall we consult her — hers the small, bright, crafty eye fixed to the keyhole
Of a door we cannot open? Shall we pull like the famished at the flowered
     stuff
Of her skirt, implore her to speak? Say: "What do you see now? Do you see a
     tall man
Crossing a road, maybe, of what might be a foreign country? Do you see
Him alive still, not lying quiet, but laughing out loud, it may be? Do you see

A young man, his voice quicker to sing, his feet quicker to dance
The light in his eye more reckless, and the words he speaks harder
Or else more tender in the mouth?")


## THE INTERRUPTION

Have they a special look to them, the men who bear love for their own soil,
So you know them at once when they pass in the street?
( There have been old men as savage, with voices that speak as clearly
As any young man's. There have been old men
Who walked to their execution with the same unshaken step.)

Herriot danced fearlessly the Frenchmen's dance,
Danced it steadily, quietly, to the subterranean music that played,
Followed its tempo as if it were thunder from brasses, music
Dropped note by note from oboe or flute, unsullied as mountain water
      falling.
Herriot danced to a tune whistled underground, to a trickle of sound
In portent, like a stream's murmur in springtime under the snow.

So are they pledged to dance, the fearless men; dance quietly, swiftly
Towards the grave. So must they dance as Mateotti, Blum, as Toller, as
      Carl von Ossietsky danced,
As Herriot, del Vayo, as Wallace, and Juan Negrin dance still,
Steadily, terribly, as the Marathon dancers dance; for men are born certain
      of the rhythm and steps,
Born certain of the tune, knowing exactly if the notes are false or true.

( Shall we sit at the table with the woman in the flowered dress,
Study the coarseness of her skin, the nostrils' pores, the mottled neck,
Remembering it is such vulgar, earthly flesh, giving no sign that here the
      spirit is
Which channels best the spirit's eloquence? For her alone tea leaves find
      tongue,
The palm unfolds. Shall we sit mute with wonder as she speaks,
Hushed for some word of life or death, and when they will return?
But she will eye you slyly across the cup, speak of a loan of money
      considered
Lost which soon will be repaid you. She will say a visit to a lawyer
Is reflected in the glass, that the advice he gives is good; that you should be
     . aware
Of intrigue in a business associate; that an elderly woman stands between
      you and what you want.
And we will look quickly across the table, our eyes echoing: *This is the
      wrong place*
*We have come to. These are not the answers that we came to hear.*
In our haste to go, we will seize up our gloves from the checkered cloth,
      push the coins
Under the plate for her. In the street we will take each other's arms
And laugh quickly, saying:
*We must have mistaken the number on the door.* )

Carson, the days are long this year. Let strength be gathered as tall-stalked
    flowers are
And carried, fresh and fragrant, in our hands. We know
In such uneasy times as these is history made, that it takes shape
As statues take their height, their pure, unswerving gaze, their classic line
    from the chaotic clay.
In days like these when peoples in migration stage the allegory of racial
    flight,
We have become articulate. When generations play the individual's tragedy
And triumph out, then we are marvelously and faithfully portrayed. Shall
    we
Despair that men we love move from the wings and take their part in
    history?
Let us say only
That their names are there.

# OCTOBER 1954

Now the time of year has come for the leaves to be burning.
October, and the month fills me with grief
For the girl who used to run with the black dogs through them,
Singing, before they burned. Light as a leaf
Her heart, and her mouth red as the sumac turning.

Oh, girl, come back to tell them with your bell-like singing
That you are this figure who stands alone, watching the dead leaves burn.
(The wind is high in the trees, and the clang of bluejay voices ringing
Turns the air to metal. This is not a month for anyone who grieves.)
For they would say that a witch had passed in fury if I should turn,
Gray-haired and brooding, and run now as I once ran through the leaves.

# SPRING

You see these halted days of March as a fixed season,
See as immutable nights with rain on the panes, when cats cry out for love.
But listen, listen: each man is a country, with both north and south, loyalty,
    treason,
Passion and its repudiation, in him; the birds of his forests hawk as well as
    dove.
He is in conflict as a country is, his opposed climates California, Texas,
    Maine
( Varied as you who look past me with glacial eyes, or else turn March to
    April when you speak my name).

Long arctic midnights of the heart are ours, and noondays when the mind
    swoons in the sun;
Our throats both parched for speech and liquid with eloquence, like
    canyons in which Colorado torrents run.
Crossing this desert, the bleak eye perceives man is both wilderness and
    cultivated land.
( In the stone soil of transient winter, roots move like the opening fingers of a
    dreamer's hand. )

Have you forgotten how soft the footstep falls on moss, how the daffodil
Unfurls like a trumpet's golden call; that lilacs, blue as the gaze of stars,
Burn in spring's firmament; that the slow, sweet yielding of the iron will
To the other's will is ecstasy longer than the Milky Way, sharper than
    Mars?
( Have you outstared the faded eyes of man's despair too long in the glass
To remember the willows' straight green hair, and the taste of onion grass? )

Now is the time for the old month to be unbuckled like a cape
And slipped from your shoulders; time for your lips to shape
My name as mine shape yours in the spring night; for your voice to say
The syllables gently, steadily, like the softly falling rain
( Quiet as you who turn toward me and do not breathe, evoking May in
    April when you speak my name).

( 1 9 5 6 )

# THE NEW EMIGRATION

*( On reading a French reporter's account of the clandestine crossings from Spain)*

They cross the frontier as their names cross your pages,
Dark-eyed, slender-throated, with tongues that have run
As mercury runs to the fever of sun. But now as I read, as I write,
They are crossing by moon, traps shut, guitars muted,
Fox-smell on the night, without passport or visa or money to ring. So they
    come
Through the trees. They are young, but they wear
Bleak masks of hunger, coats tight in the armpits, too short in the sleeve.
But hope can be cloak, can be shoes on the feet, can be lash
Out of bull-hide still tough in the dust when the trumpets are done.

The joke of it is they are not in the news. Not Koreans who follow torrent
    and stone
From northward to southward; not Germans who flux from east toward the
    west.
These quick-eyed, these young, who are musical-tongued, have blood that
    is lava
Pursuing the vein from lover to lover, Spaniard to Spaniard, dead man to
    son,
And no milestone to say it is here, the frontier.

But the dead of wars and hunger rattling in their beds
Are stilled in the brief, sweet moment that the thin-ribbed come
Out of the province of Zamora, out of Asturias, Seville,
Bearing in flight their country, bearing Spain,
Leaving the soft-voweled names behind to genuflection; not to bend
Elbow or knee again, but to cross before the altars of wild olive trees,
Upright, like men.
Here France is France, wide open in the dark,
Who takes them in.

Does history state that all men seek the classical
Grave face of liberty, leave interchangeable footprints as they run,
Communicate identical dreams from man to son,
Whatever the continent or century? Listen. Men

Are as different as their climates are. The pride of some
Lies in the passage of firearms from palm to palm,
War after war, along an iron Rhine; in some
The honeycomb has hardened like an artery. But not in these
Whose presence states a frontier is that undetermined place
One comes upon alone at night, in life, and crosses
Even if afraid.

(1956)

# DREAMS DREAMED

Spring birds wing to the feeding tray
As Bowery bums wing to a bar. Their wings
Are slick as worn-out sleeves. They sing,
Both birds and bums, melodiously and grievously.
Their feet are thin. Both species wing
To seed and drink with lidless eyes.

Could I but strew in with the sunflower seeds
That wild beaks seek, the dreams
Contained within the eggshell skulls of bums,
Would I not be both bird and bum, and seed and drink,
And grief and melody? Would I not see
With equal clarity the morning star,
And the glass left empty at the corner bar?

(1958)

# A POEM OF GRATITUDE

*for Caresse Crosby*

Now the tide is coming in, each long, low, hastening wave in the cove
Arching a little, barely spuming, but running
Into the salt grass the way a river whispers in.
I see the fluid fingers pass along the shallows
And the scalpel of the jetty probing, and you are far
In ether-sleep, the small door of your heart first swinging wide,
Then closing, opening and closing, hinged not by tissue, but by metal
In their quick, gloved hands. I think of you,
Tender as spring fern in the rain, pliant as seaweed
In man's current. I see the waves ride swiftly in
On the sands, see the weather vane reel on its pole,
Its fluctuating arrow crying: Here, here, there is breath!
And I say: This is good, it must be good, this omen. I have known
The meridian of your heart too long, too long,
To accept any break in it, any crack, any faltering.

Now the far star of the lighthouse shines,
And the moon floats in the trees, rosy and silken. The waves run softly in,
And the nighthawk gives its brief, fierce cry
As you once cried. Where you now lie, the tide of ether ebbs,
And the small door of your heart opens and closes, opens,
But now it is the south wind of your blood that fans it wide.

In the clear dusk, I put my arm around the memory of all we were,
Of all we were not, and I am happy,
Watching the cove hold in its curve the deepening waters of the tide.

(1958)

# TWO TWILIGHTS
## FOR WILLIAM CARLOS WILLIAMS

Here where I live
The birds speak in a shower of voices
In the trees at dusk, taking
Sweet-tongued decisions about north or south,
Or near or far,
The evening stillness fluid with
These liquid tongues
That run like silver water to
The island of the heart.

Both twilights bring this multitudinous whispering
Across the cove,
A music spuming from the quiet leaves
At dawn, at dusk. Here in the open window
The stars fade as the first birds' voices call,
The birds' tongues cease at the coming of the stars.

(1959)

Tall birds have come into the cove tonight. Not swans,
But bittern and loon and black-legged egret, printing their words on the
    wet sand.
Unlike bird crying to bird, this stenciled tongue, or wind to sea,
Or wave calling hollowly to land; rather a whispered dialogue their cold feet
    trace,
Claw, nail, and spur, laid cautiously on sand bereaved of tide,
The silence of this they have said, or sought to say, brittle with grit,
Immediately effaced. Even the brooding ire of the small blue heron dies.

You have written of starling and finch, killdeer and plover, having seen
    them
In meadow, on bough, in the hills, quick-winged, with cover to take,
Unlike these tall, bent, bleak-eyed men who walk,
Separate as poets, stating their confirmation of man's nomad place.
"Do not make it a history of statesmen and generals," you said, with the
    bulb overhead
Lighting your face. "Save it, for God's sake, from dates, wars, kings"; not
    saying then:

"Maybe more like the words the birds' feet trace in the cove at night.
It does not matter if the sands close over them."

(1959)

# A NIGHT LETTER

I shall not see your face for so long now

                                      longer longer

Than the long vines of arbutus leading
March into April    April into May
Or see your hands

                              ( save in the portrait I have painted )
The south wind of their tenderness unfolding
Newest leaf and frailest root and smallest grain
                        ( the right hand being sun   the left hand rain )

I shall not see you who blasphemed the nights

                                  stamped out the stars

Waking to each morning's bright chastising
Piecing the fragments of the hours that remain
Into sternest clearest shape again

                               carefully redesigning
Forenoons and noons to lucid symmetry

It will be long long before I see your face again

                              .        oh longer

Than any length of summer or the long blue dusks
In which your image burns

                           your face the brightest fire
So you blaze

                     in the spring and autumn of the seasons' change
Speak in the far far sighing of the mourning dove
Stir in the unicorn's long exquisite dying

                            ( 1 9 6 0 )

# RENDEZVOUS

We have met in the cafés of two countries
                              Vayo
There will be others
                    Walked
The Boulevard of Nasturtiums under
The tall rains of Montmartre
From the Pont Neuf watched
The faces within the current
Passing turning
Their dead mouths not crying out

We have seen the guards of white
Lilac change from green bud to flower
At the glass doors of Jeu de Paumes
                              Tuileries
                                   Bagatelle
Viewed there the ocher the blue
The shaggy grasses of van Gogh
                    (But behind the pictures the lilacs the rains
There is a wall always a·wall and
The blindfolded stand against it
                         They fling
Their shadows to us like dark cloaks
As they fall)

In the rue St. Honoré café
                         Vayo
She read the language of lines
                         Head
Stronger than heart
Heart eloquent as head
                    Recall
The gypsy saw on the heel of your thumb a tracery
Of government buildings
                    Granite or marble?
I asked and where is the country?
Eager as history to hear it said

                    ( Recall
Her skirts were two sunsets one yellow
For rain the other good omen for
Sailors at evening blazing red )
                              It is
Over land not over water it is
Not far she said


The bugles of headlines blow in the gutter
                              Vayo
Green-lidded girls pale-mouthed with nun's black
Narrowed to ankle and thigh stroll past
It is the Village the day is summer when I say
                              Vayo Vayo
The sound of it echoes against bleakest stone
                              ( for each street
We walk is prison hall is courtyard wall
                              at morning
The blindfolded fling their shadows to us
Like dark wings as they fall )


                              ( 1961 )

# A WINTER FABLE

Salzburg is like a crystal palace in the winter
Christmas eve the time to go there
With bells in ears even if the heart
Grieves an old woman quaking in a shawl
On Mozart's doorstep asking that his hand
Dispense his gold turn light upon the keys again
And still again illuminate those rooms in which the threads of music
Spindled revolve the stage-sets bright as
Separate fires kindled

There is another stage so hot in color
That the eyes cry curtain curtain curtain
But it will not fall
Act after act they mime their toothless roles
Without foyer or remission without program five
Or six old hags cast up against the wainscoting
Of Grand Central's ladies' room the shifting
Tide of others comes and goes using the lavabos
The central grandness of their lives discarding
Those without train-time or destination the hags
With legs as gnarled as Christmas stockings
Packed with varicose veins instead of presents
Their shoes split to allow their bunions
To take the air this place
That offers heat and light for nothing
Has become their salon the trains stammer
Accompaniment to their silent guffawing
Here they entertain the creaking dreams
Of youth malodorous by this time here
Pour tea from thermos bottles with the
Vacuum lining shattered like the moon on water
The tin casing decorated with safety pins
Necklaces of paper clips with pages
From the Bible torn in four and stapled
Tea laced with a shot of something else not very
Savory their invisible guests no more
Nor less than the inebriated wraiths of

– what? Try to say it without the mouth
Splitting the face with grinning from ear
To ear even the letters of the alphabet refuse
To spell it
> (I swear if I was a man I'd wait
> With orchids at that stage door with "Ladies"
> Written above the portal I'd take them home
> The lot of them establish them
> In solace these with the cumbersome shape
> Of mothers the three categories of mother
>> the neglected
>>> the long forgotten
>>> and the dead)

It was eleven o'clock on this particular Christmas eve when a neatly dressed Negro lady came in to the ladies' waiting room, pulling behind her a little wagon made out of a packing box and painted red. It had bright black wire-spoked wheels, this snappy little wagon, and a long flexible chromium shaft by which the lady, neat as a needle, guided it over the damp and odorous tiles. In the wagon, on a cushion, sat a cat with the head of a male ballet dancer. His coat was finer than satin, and his markings were such that he appeared to wear a dark hood drawn low upon his brow. At the sight of this cat in the wagon, the eyes of the five or six old hags returned from the vast Saharas of the past, from the wide reaches of catastrophe, and halted at this oasis, bitter as arsenic, the waters of it, if they only knew.

"Now, Leonard, you just take a look around and make up your mind," the Negro lady said. She had the look of a schoolteacher about her, perhaps because of the finicky statement of her dark blue outfit and the gold-rimmed spectacles she wore. Not even the lacy white wool scarf laid over her hair could take the edge of discipline away. She was made out of flat narrow laths, or so it seemed, so thin you would think she was starving to death, only nobody starves in New York City (not even the Bowery bum who died last week standing upright in a doorway. He didn't starve, he froze to death, the newspaper said, although the autopsy showed he hadn't eaten since several days).

"Leonard's a boy of discrimination. You know that, Mrs. Morgan," the Negro lady was saying to the ladies'-room attendant. "You know as well as I do that he'll always pick out the nicest-looking lady in the place, and I don't mean empty prettiness. He looks for character." The cat had an emerald leather collar around his licorice neck, and he was chained to the wagon by a nickel chain. He lowered his head like a cobra and peered at the ladies who came and went in front of the mirrors, running combs through their hair, shaking the cinders of Pittsburgh or Chicago, or the sands of Atlantic City, out of their locks, and putting something else quickly in its place so that nobody would know.

The hags were immobile as Christmas stockings spiked to the chimney piece, and the eyes of the chipper travelers were fixed on the swinging doors of the cabinays, hoping to slither their buxom forms in without benefit of dime dropped in the slot. One of these was so dressed that she looked like two bloated leopards stitched together. There she stood, buttoned short and broad and irate in her painted plush, elbowing her way through the accumulated others, upbraiding her own reflection in fury before she recognized it was herself before her, outraged with passion in the glass.

"I'm just letting you take your time, Leonard. You know that," the Negro lady said to the cat. They did not offer romance, friendship, or any of the popular commodities, but in the end they possessed the entire scene. She had now grown a stick (like Aaron's rod) from her right hand, and she tapped the cat on the shoulder with the tip of it. "Leonard, you're being very choosy tonight. Sometimes he makes up his mind in a minute," she said, and she flicked at him sharply with the cane. When she touched him thus, the satin skin of his shoulder jerked, and he peered with gold-eyed gravity at the women who had now begun to gather close. It was clear to all he was seeking something different from what he saw. Let me tell you that the stick was like a vein through which the power of the Negro lady's narrow will sought vainly to pass into the cat. "Sometimes he'll jump right down and start sloping around," she was saying as she whacked him with the stick again. "Leonard," she said, and her voice was rising, "you just pick out the lady who looks nicest to you, and you tell us what you think of her. We're all waiting on you, Leonard," she said.

"Rainy days she'll bring him in here and he'll have a yellow slicker on, and a rain hat tied under his chin," said the ladies'-room attendant. "He has a bunch of fortunes in that little bag on the seat. He chooses a lady, and she gives him a little something, and then she gets her fortune all printed out." "A little something?" cried the woman whose squat and terrible body the bloated leopards were constantly devouring. "Maybe a quarter," said the attendant. "Nobody can tell if he's going to pick out a young girl or a woman wise in the ways of love," said the Negro lady. "It's class he's interested in."

> Beyond the circle of women who pressed close
> The hags sat on the leather benches
> Sat against the wainscoting sat
> With their haunches quivering sat
> Their eyes opaque believing that
> Now with sleigh bells in the ears
> Frost on the lashes now with the arteries
> Of Christmas hardening justice was about
> To be meted out.

The old women were ready to take
Their uppers and lowers out of their
Handbags and clamp them in their jaws again
Were dying to frizz the strands
Of their lank hair between forefinger
And thumb to push their legs out of sight
Under the ruptured benches if only
He would look their way
If he had stretched one paw one claw
The toothpick or fishbone of a whisker in their
Direction they would have taken the
Withered masks from their faces and let
The tears of self-pity, gratitude (synonymous
With greed and lust) fall from
Their orbs.

"Oh, I know him well, the crafty puss!" said his mistress while the women watched. "He looks so frank and honest, doesn't he, with that topaz stare! I tell you he'll do this sometimes just to drive me to cut my throat! Leonard!" she cried out sharply, but he did not move. He sat, sleek and competent in his ballet dancer's black silk tights and his smooth imitation sealskin hood, wanting none of what he saw. "You jump right down now and go to the lady you think is the nicest here tonight. You go and do it, Leonard, and maybe she'll give you a quarter, or if you choose right, fifty cents. It's Christmas, Leonard!" But what did he do instead but turn on his cushion and lie down, drawing the glossy rope of his tail around his elbows, and narrowing his shoulders so that they need bear no responsibility.

"That's your decision, is it? Then no liver tomorrow, Leonard!" said the Negro lady, and her voice was tight and small. Suddenly she lifted the stick and struck the cat five cracking blows. It seemed his spine must break in two from the force of the stick, but it did not break, nor did he writhe like a half-killed cobra in the waiting-room dirt. Instead, he cringed in a corner of the wagon, flat as a cockroach, his eyes gone black with mourning for the dignity she had taken away. "So you aren't going to choose anyone tonight? So nobody's good enough for Leonard, is that it?" she shouted, and she struck at his skull. But now he reared up on his hind legs and fought the cane, while the circle of women moved away.

> The water ran into the basins
> The toilets flushed and
> Mrs. Morgan picked up
> The dripping mop and pushed it
> Across the floor the hags
> Watched from the benches watched
> And took their thermos bottles out
> To offer drinks to wraiths that
> Twisted on the air they watched
> The Negro lady strike
> At the cat's quick subtle life
> Now become the bone and flesh of what
> They once had been neat-ankled silken-haired
> Their red gums grinning at the Negro lady
> As attrition and the cat the shackled will.

(1960)

# POEMS FOR A PAINTER

## POEM FOR A PAINTER WHO DRINKS WINE

If you could shape in stone the thing you seek
Through interchangeable tongues through labyrinth
Of faces breasts as similar as stars as unattainable
As white what distant place you look to without name
What lonely height
You flee by planet hurricane by moon
From one man's restless bed outwitting him to intercept
His hands and mouth at rest in tender hair shout
Outraged elegy and chant and fable of anemone
Not finding him asleep in any woman's cycle or outgoing tide's
Alone the tireless self barefooted runs from stair to stair
Crying aloud
   not there
     not there
       not there

          (1960)

## PRINT FROM A LUCITE BLOCK

Last night as I crossed
The black ice toward your image
A deer ran.

The fume of his breath fled
As he leapt sprang ran
Bearing the constellations
On his high branched head.

And my heart like the deer
Asked that carrot fern, turnip, fresh greens
Proffer their leaves despite the month
The time of year.

The words to say this were mute spears
That had been running water once and ceased.
In the night's cracked glass
Your image turned from shadow to moonlight
As the antlered deer leapt past.

(1961)


## SEASCAPE FOR AN ENGRAVER

You are the far
                    far figure straying there
Against the tide you
                    are the footprint filled with sea
Marking the desolation
                    of the cold sands
                                silently

You are the drift from moorings
                                the tormented prow
Of those who know the perilous name
                                of distance and pronounce it savagely

You are more distant sadder
                                than the farthest star
Circles of water widen
                    from the mute small core
The sea-filled footprint
                    that you are

But through my lashes
                    swiftest tears devise
A tremulous rainbow arched
To where you stand
                    engraving
The frail shadow of man's long prevailing
                                with knife with burin
Or with empty hand

(1961)

# THE ARTIST SPEAKS....

## (BELLIGERENTLY)

So, nightly, hourly, I violate my mind,
And ravish the images as they appear.
What's it to you? My art's for me a seizing of my own reality!

There is no measure of time in art, no long year matters.
Being an artist means to reckon and count, but also to be
Like the tree which does not force its sap, its leaves,
But stands without tremor in the storms of spring,
Not fearing that summer may refuse to come.
I tell you summer comes, God damn it! I have seen her yellow hair!

Nothing that belongs to another should befall us, only what has long been
    ours
Within the narrow corridors of stamping blood.
I am unique, not repeatable,
Born in rebellion, still being that which at every turning of my life I was!

## .... THE WOMAN ANSWERS

## (SOFTLY)

But gently, gently as lips across the face the whisper is:
The sea forever loses all that it embraces.
It cannot prolong ecstasy or fear.

Patience, humility, like daffodils in April,
Withstand the seasons of your black despair,
Their faces wet with rain, trembling until
Your violent hand returns to find them there.

But must not remain, believing that all your sadnesses are moments of
    illusion;
That the solitary has no distance, that all measures change.
Whisper that nothing alters, the rod, the single prick of thistle,

The arrow are the same; the point,
The shaft, the lance, the finger,
Planted within a long green evening stillness
Take root and give endurance to your name.

(1960)

## THE PAINTER SPEAKS —
## THE WOMAN ANSWERS

the attempt to be a painter and nothing but a painter finding AM so difficult
that an abandonment comes so difficult that an abandonment

(Sweet brother painter, this is a lullaby for the abandoned. This is a cradle
song for those who turn at night to watch sleep running through the hands)

the attempts of life and the attempts of art the claims of each on the other
endlessly separating AM endlessly separating

(This is an afternoon in April. The stream is a needle running through fab-
ric of watercress and green frog voices, making once piece of wind and land.
Hear the child's words quick as crickets jumping: "Ecoutes, Maman, c'est
le printemps! Ecoutes les peepers! C'est le commencement de la vie encore
une fois!")

an awareness comes deeply an awareness comes of the fight others fought
that begins and begins and once begun so difficult that an abandonment
comes an abandonment comes

(Then drink waltzes in to the shrill bagpiping of the stars, the thundering
drums of the blood stampeding. But after, after, even the young hand trem-
bles in the dawn with cold, even the young mouth breaks with weeping)

what am I AM? is AM a tragic fusion becoming continually but never quite
becoming AM?

(It is one man not two who walks into a room, makes the chairs take hands
and dance, brings violets to flower, lettuce hearts and avocados leap to green
for spring)

Christ the other sleeps snores cries out the foul room turning painter or man
or neither let him lie

(1961)

## The Evening Grass

They have an innocence the words
*Take your own life*
Or *took his life*
As if they spoke of your or his accumulated days
Taken in casual accounting walking through
The evening grass no graver not so grave as if
Either you or he had turned and taken
An indifferent woman in the evening grass
But life does not
Go out this quietly not whispering not
Murmuring through the grass but
Differently so differently
You heard
The blast his dying made

Know it was not for him alone you wept
And not for him the endless pounding
Of the flagstones with a mallet's wood until
The skulls of all men broke that
Dusk until the splintering was your brain's
Glass and his memory's crockery
You ran
The jagged staircase of your grief for all
Who say tonight
tonight
tonight
Yes LIFE tonight to liquid ears and no
One hears it was for paintings out of frames that

Lean on warehouse walls for all
The lost engravings of the heart wild
Cardiographs of lust you wept for flesh
That had not lingered in his bed for mouths
That did not lie upon his mouth
                              The tide of brine
From eyes and nose roared through the
Seaweed of the evening grass star flowers stayed
While pounding pounding with one hand you flung
The wooden arms of trees upon
The flame their brittle fingers snapping
As they burned Christ let the pyre burn you wept
Burn burn
                              Burn far beyond

This place this year into
A clearing where the blackened soul can stand
Green-leafed and rooted still
                              *He took his life*

Is quiet as breathing
It makes hardly any sound


                              ( 1 9 6 1 )

# TWO POEMS FOR A POET

If I told you the trees spoke, there being no wind
That night, no sighing of branches, you would say
Well, there was outcry, but hardly, hardly,
Syntax, not leaves or pine needles falling in syllables
Or tears, indistinguishable one from the other, but
Eloquent, green. No; there were none of these.

Yet I tell you they spoke. The trees' sap
Ebbed to the roots faster than any dying tide,
And timber, rigid as kindling, followed the bleak
Cortege of November out of season, dry
In the orchard by your house. The trees,
Their language a cackling of blighted leaves,
Abjured the willows grieving by the water.
Apple or peach flower no longer drifted down.
Strangled by mistletoe, as if in winter,
Their forked summits black, high, unbroken, they
Trembled in the bright blizzard of the April stars.

But they had died, the trees, and they were felled, their lean
Knotted fingers holding back their cries. They were split
To firewood, their pulp consumed, and in the cold ashes
Of their vanishing — I cannot tell you how — the trees
Found supple root again, and, sweet-mouthed, spoke
In voices of young nuns, of novices, not veiled
But certain beyond bewilderment of spring's intent. Their
Lips passed sentence, but so pure, so final
In its innocence that sap rose, fresh as evening,
In the throats, the tongues, the limbs, of these dark, slender trees
And answered with April clarity whatever leafless question had been asked.

How quiet must be the road where
You walk this morning. How greenly springing
The grass as you go through the sun.
The birds must call like a currency of silver ringing,
And the high winged singing of the heart
Must rise in the breast.

I would like to be near you in the early walking
And hear not the birds' jubilation, or the heart's,
But the sadder, sadder sound
Of the poet talking.

(1961)

# A SQUARE DANCE FOR A SQUARE

This time the accordions will cry out – not me, for I'll start laughing.
Now that I've learned the Left Square Through,
The Texas Star, the Dip'n Dive, I'm armed with you. I
Won't trip on my three-tiered skirt, but Half Sashay
And Back Track with an Inside Out, an Outside In. I'll
Box the Flea, Shoot That Star, do a Courtesy Turn toward
Where you are. I will not fall and crack my skull, neither
My jaw nor my buckling knee.

To square dance is to stomp, to clap, to yodel out
One's terror. It is a segregated rite, the
Opposite number of the minstrel show. And you, sweet partner
Of men's furtive nights, you Do Sa Do, shuffling but law-abiding,
Warily do the Wrong Way Thar and Cross Trail Through.

> And then
> > and then

The intermission comes, returning you
To the pitch and howl of long back alleys
Where the cool cats stray. Above the roofs, past
Known identity, the far stars tremble at their own imaginings,
The shook blood draws a likeness that you
Rip in two. You bring me Hawaiian Sunlight in a paper cup,
Sickened with vitamins, and turn away, taking your fingers
With you, "Hey," I say, "hey, hey! Shuffle
A little longer!" But silence is the numb blue baby
Clutched against your stamping breast. You walk
The parquet flooring of your life with it, stick
A cigar between its gums, throttle it on lighter fluid,
Whisper to it: "Hush, hush, God damn you." But it can't stop.
It's silence already. Who can shut his trap on silence anyway?

There is a curtain that divides your life. The members
Of the cast who have no lines to say
Clamor behind its folds, grimace, and point; and you before it,
Blinded by footlights, uneasily play

The Eight Chain Thru. I cannot
See from where I am, cannot applaud. My hands
Are tied, finger to finger, like a nun's
In prayer. Not upright in the aisle, and not in loge,
Not hunched in gallery, I watch you cross the boards
With lowered head, the shoulders stooped
To guard the heart from onslaught, the body hollowed
Like a palm to hold the measure of outrage you claim.

         Shuffler,
They are not yours, the griefs, deaths, losses, burials of
Other men. Neither the See Saw nor the Wagon Wheel describes
Your gait, but something else, something like seeing you walk
A road made luminous by moon at night, each ankle
Dragging with it ball and chain.

   And then
     and then

Your anger stops the music suddenly, rips the accordion in two, snaps
The catgut of fiddle, extracts the piano's teeth from wooden gums
Without a cry. "The dancing has stopped," I say.
"The square dance is finished," I whisper as you walk away.

You slept once in a field, close by the lake, and there
In sleep you spoke their names. They came, crowding the grass,
Tougher than daisies, than thistles, than Queen Anne's Lace, until
There was no space for breath. And I that day was every face
That turned toward you: I, the child-hustler from 42nd Street,
Trying the skeleton key in your apartment door, asking to enter
The back bedroom of your despair; I, the illicit roomer with
Briefcase and lowered girlish lids who once, in sleep, had kissed
You on the mouth; and I, the Negro mounting the stairs
Two at a time, for fear, for fear; and I, Brother Infidelious
With glossy hair, pacing the cloistered vineyards of your diocese,
Telling my beads, a girl's high heels beneath
The cassock's hem. Mine were the heels, and mine
The voice that murmured at times in blasphemy, at times in prayer.
I was that workman in the Philadelphia bar, the place dark as a mine
Though it was noon, the underground explosion, the catastrophe

Within the heart or pit already taken place. At the bleak shaft
The women and the unborn children stood, and I was every wife and every
Toothless, bereft hag, and every child who cried your name. While you
Black-masked and mute, asked nothing except of one man, skinny and
 quick
As a mosquito, seated at the bar, with legs drawn up to strike the venom in;
And I, without the flicker of an eyelash, became him.

But there was the leaping of great rabbits once
In the summer, the splashing of lake fish in the sun.
There was the square dance of tombstones
On needles of frost one November. But never again, never again.
You laughed out loud at the calls: "Allemande Left
Your corner, partner right. Those in the center retain the Star
But release the hands of those outside, then four couples right
And now Left Through, Dixie Grand, and a
Do Paso, Frontier Whirl, and Catch All Eight. Couple Wheel Around
And Weave That Ring, Weave Around, don't touch a thing. Four Couples
Susie-Q, bow to your partner, your corner, too,
Wave to the girl across from you." The caller says: "You're doing fine!"
As I crack my skull, my jaw, my knee, when you take
Your hand away from mine.

(1963)

# THUNDERSTORM IN SOUTH DAKOTA

All that blazing day, swift-breasted swallows, envious crows, grackles in
     trees,
Gathered in roadside conference. At dusk
Winged ants splattered the windshield, dying indelibly.
No ripped glove, no kleenex, could efface their gauze
From the glass. At night, on the black pass, the bereft
Sheep slept, and I, bereft, was awakened by fountains of light
Spraying over the granite monuments of clouds, over the towers and
     cornices,
Over this toppling architecture of storm,
And I wrote you:

"I am afraid of the uproar of this demolition,
And reach my hand out in the alien motel bed,
Seeking all that is absent, seeking the pulse
That skips so lightly in your wrist. I remember
The singular wisdom of your hands, their shape,
Their knowledge of many things, the narrow division of your fingers.
It is so different, this thundering of stone, this clamor, this that pounds at
     the window,
Drenching the beasts in their stretches of land on the South Dakota pass;
It is so different from the uncertain pace of your heart, from the far rain,
That is falling, falling, gentle as tears, in Ireland where you are."

(1965)

# A SHORT POEM IN COLOR

Damn it, one shouts, but there is no echo in the forest
For the temper pales with the years; it is no longer
Metal writhing red in the foundry
Of whose impatience, yours or mine?
As one grows old, the hair need not be combed so often
For the wind no longer seizes it
With wild trembling hands.
These things I have read in books,
But I have not been told what season swings
Its searchlight white across the skunk dark of
Philanderings, driving the shadows – black cattle in panic –
Down back ways where men (say men who have refused the midday
Illumination of fidelity) relieve themselves against promiscuous stone
Despite God's admonition scrawled across the granite wall:
*"Mes pauvres enfants, défense d'uriner."*

(1965)

# A POEM ABOUT THE JEWS

I have had enough of them, more than enough;
Enough of the pages allotted to them, the margins
Crowded with faces, not as high ground is thronged
With sheep whose lips tear at the parched grass
Between stones, but crowded as subway platforms are
With a mosaic of faces, eloquent beyond lamentation
In the rush hour of returning home.
I have had enough of the silent chapters
Of their history. ("Without outcry"
Is written in every language of their coming and going.)
I am sick and tired of every word of it. And you, you haven't
The time to listen, so do not listen. There is so much else to do.

> After some centuries had passed
> The descendants of Abraham
> Took on the bright density of tribes,
> Related not only by common worship
> But by common ancestry. (So they began.)
> Crop failures and droughts—the skeleton
> Hand of the parched wind sifting the dust—
> Impelled them to ask, as other nomads had asked,
> Leave to pasture their flocks in the western fringes
> Of the Nile's tidal mouth.
> There, on slopes cropped by the square teeth of
> Sheep, goats, occasional donkeys,
> Following highways of emerald bulrushes,
> Water to their anklebones, bearded,
> These shepherds roamed. They sojourned
> A long while in Egypt, speaking their own tongue,
> Compliant, peaceful as saints, and were
> In acknowledgment reduced to servitude.
> (Such was their lot.) They who had been freemen,
> Their spirits illuminated by loneliness,
> Became bondsmen, groaning under
> The taskwork of fashioning bricks
> From the gold mud slipping under foot,
> Bemoaned their destiny as they built Pithom and Ramses,

East of Goshen (cities without subways to herd them
Or housing projects to take them in), crying out
In longing for those places where the name Israel
Lived still, was still whispered on the dunes,
However far.

You have heard all this before.
You know that on one occasion a shepherd wandered
Deeper into the wilderness seeking fresher valleys, and passed
Close by the mountain of Horeb, of Sinai; and there beheld a bush alight.
But neither the branches of that bush nor the frail white flowers
Were devoured by the flame. However fiercely they burned,
They did not burn. The shepherd, a little slow of tongue,
Slow of thought even, it is rumored, could find
No explanation for this miracle (in the presence of which
The flocks stood ruminating) until a clear voice spoke in the rush hour
Of the return. The God of the fathers called out from the fire.
It was twilight. There were no stars yet
To bear witness, no clouds to veil the planets had they appeared.
The evening was blue as sapphire, translucent as amethyst.
There was silence
Except for the voice that spoke. It bade
The shepherd lead his people into freedom.
You know how the exodus took place in the petalled springtime
Of the year one thousand two hundred and twenty
Before Christ's name was known.

And then, to go on with it, in 1093, Peter the Hermit,
A native of Picardy, set forth on pilgrimage to Jerusalem,
And in wrath at the miseries of the pilgrims
Returned to Europe, crying out that the duty of the Church
Was the deliverance of the holy places from the infidel.
In Mayence, the Crusaders passed, and the Jews had trouble.
"The blood of the men mingled with the blood of their wives,"
It is written, "and the strong, sad blood of the fathers
Mingled with their children's blood;
The blood of the brothers with their sisters', the
Blood of the teachers with their disciples', the
Blood of the grooms with their brides', the
Blood of the judges with their scribes', the

Blood of the infants with their mothers'."
(We know all this, the wailing, the bemoaning,
Centuries without end.)
But one thing more, just one,
And then I'll keep quiet about it.
In July 1099, the knights in tunics
Of chain and coats of mail, and the riffraff
That accompanied them, captured Jerusalem.
Godfrey of Boulogne was made king; and thus
Was founded the Latin kingdom of Jerusalem
Whose life, it is recorded, "was one of the most painful
Ever penned; a history of almost unredeemed envy,
Malice, shame; a kingdom that in eighty-eight years
Would disappear as suddenly as it had come, leaving no trace
Save the ruins of castles and churches,
And the countless dead; save a few place names
And a deathless legacy: the hatred of Christianity
In the hearts and the marrow of the natives there."

But let me keep history straight.
"The ears of him who hears these things will tingle,
For who has ever heard anything like this?" wrote Solomon bar Samson
Early in his century, asking the question much too soon;
For presently Edessa fell to the Mohammedans, and Pope Eugenius,
Poor man, beside himself, out of his wits, doing his utmost,
Issued a call for a new Crusade. In response to the fiery eloquence
Of St. Bernard, multitudes gathered about the King of France,
About the German Emperor, and again the Jews stretched out their necks.
(That is the ancient phrase for it.) They thrust forth
Their necks and let the bright knife find its place.
The Germans were not alone in their fury. There were always
The others. There were the virtuous, happy, just, ecclesiastical men,
The pompous, the titled, the revered, of France, England, Spain, all
Those who trembled at the look of features different from their own.
The Germans were not alone — except as each man's judgment of himself
Is secret and isolate, and has no nation's name. The bishops, delicate of
        thought,
Acute of sensibility, sought to protect the outcasts. St. Bernard himself
Permitted no excesses. Christian usurers, he argued, were no better
Than Jewish usurers. (That was gracious of him.) But still Jews,

He made clear, should remit interest due from such of those
Who took the Cross.

    At this moment in the wearisome history,
    In the furtive annals on which no light of day, but only
    Gaslight flickers, the instigator was the monk Radulph,
    A pious man, gentle with birds, who in his devotion
    Skipped in monk's attire along the Rhine,
    Preaching that Jews living in the cities and villages
    Should be effaced; like vermin, he specified,
    Like rats; for were not their eyes as avid,
    Their noses twice as long? His teachings
    Bore fruit, and among the hundreds who were quickly slain
    ( Or who took their children's lives and then their own) was Simeon,
    The Saint of Treves, returning on foot from England, making his
        way
    Along the high road, where, not far from Cologne,
    In the Queen Anne's Lace and the dust,
    He was done to death by the passing noblemen of that Crusade.

( Young men and young women shall not dance together,
Wrote Judah, the mystic from Italy, the Jewish saint,
But each sex shall dance by itself. No Jew, so his
Teachings went, shall disguise himself in the garments
Of a Christian cleric to escape persecution, or shall
He sew a cross upon his cloak.) I can hear you sighing.
I too have no patience left for the regulations of history:
"Jews to move freely, and carry their wares from
Place to place, but not to settle; Jews to hold no
Public offices, inasmuch as they have been
Condemned in expiation to perpetual slavery; Jews
To wear a special dress, or a distinctive sign,
A badge to be pinned or embroidered on their
Garments, a star, yellow in color, over the perfidious heart."
All this happened a long time ago. It's closed
In the pages of books "without outcry." Even the
Equalities they attained are like far, alien music,
Scarcely played: "No toll to be levied on
A Jewish corpse when removed from one city to another, from
One province to another." Cannot the burden finally be laid down?

No, not quite yet, not quite yet. Something has happened.
It is much later. It is July 1964. There are two hundred sailors,
Maybe three hundred, wooden clubs in their hands to fight off rattlesnakes,
Water moccasins. They move through the suck of the Mississippi
    swamplands,
Wearing hip boots as they comb the bayous. They drag the Pearl River
( Which yields other bodies, dismembered, bloated, but not those of the two
    Jews
And the Catholic who had left no sign.) The frogs and the varmints hush
    their throbbing
As the skiffs paddle in, the orchestra moaning again once
The searchers have passed. It is said that one of the three died
Because of the beard he wore and the shape of his features. It is said
The state ordered coats of armor buckled on to meet the invasion of
    "Jews and other scum."
It is said that Choctaw Indians saw the mob gathering; but Indians
Have been sent back through time to the beginning. They no longer have a
    tongue.
The air was heavy with magnolia, light with the smell of honeysuckle.
The land for miles around was silent. The night they lay warm in the
    southern earth,.
The bush did not burn. There was no miracle. Yet their names were
    spoken,
Jewish names, shepherds like the other, Goodman and Schwerner,
And one who was Catholic, Chaney, their faces eloquent
Beyond lamentation in the rush hour of returning. Can we say
Now we have heard enough? Can we say the history is done?

(1965)

# A POEM FOR ARTHUR

You shook the liquid amber tree
And all my earrings fell
From it. Letters had come
From everyone, from
Taxi drivers, homing pigeons, B. J. Chute,
And other members of the National Institute.
My acute despair about one earring
Extinguished the candles of Marianne's birthday cake.
"The earring's lost, the dinner's off!" she cried,
And the Academy elevators rose and fell.
(She sent me a ten-dollar bill to buy another —
Earring, not dinner. She spoke
With delicacy of the eucalyptus leaves,
Emerald and dark on my white dress.) But nothing
Came of it until you shook the liquid amber
Tree outside the door, and the pods fell,
Raining their seeds into your scarlet beard,
Into your hair, and I believed then
That earrings have a season, that if you stood
A long time in the rain
There would be earrings, white as hawthorn,
Lying as in Tiffany's on the mauve satin
Of the afternoon. I believed
The candles on the birthday cake would spring to flame
Again, a finger of icing tracing "Marianne —
Marianne Moore," the thirteen letters of her name.

(1965)

# THE LOST DOGS OF PHNOM PENH

Do not stab my heart like this, scabby vagrants, garbage hounds, waiting
For the truck to sail on its tide of odor into port.
At one-thirty in the morning (now, as then), truck wheels are hushed by
    the monsoon rains
Or the clamor of the Asian stars, and you are there. You have
No growl in throat, no snarl on lip, you do not shout names at one another,
Death, the ineluctable, being so near. You wait on brittle haunches, dream
Of the fine enamel of eggshells not quite scraped of their contents; of
A strip of lettuce glistening with the solid gold of oil.

Back in this land of packaged meats, at one-thirty in the morning (now, as
    then),
I think of you, of your ribs curved like the wicker of crickets' cages,
The desiccated crickets of your hearts no longer chirping behind the bars.
I think of you, lost dogs, of the eternal wishbones of your breasts.
Under the streetlights you form a motley alphabet,
Unsuitable for use in any language. When one of you lies down,
He draws the wooden links of a tail around his elbows.
His body shapes a weary "m," humped like a camel, in defeat.
Another of you becomes the letter "u," like a sick lamb curved across the
    shepherd's
Forearm. But nowhere among you can I find a "t," high as a whistle keening
Beyond the reach of human ear; nowhere among you is there an "e,"
The beginning of that ironic "enough." I seek these letters
To complete the brief word "mute" that is closed, fleshless,
Bloodless, in the cold anvils of your jaws. At one-thirty in the morning,
The radio in my kitchen tells me that America, my country, is the garbage
    capital of the world.

Lost dogs of Phnom Penh, cry out, cry out, as men cry out
Across the intricate frontier of broken, still unbroken, Vietnam,
Under the same unfaltering stars!

(1966)

# A POEM OF LOVE

The day you told me you had a bank account
Of inestimable proportions, too great
For balancing in any checkbook,
More multitudinous than the loose silver of the Milky Way,
I entered without genuflection the crypt, the bank vault,
Of the forest, trod moss softer than folding money,
At the cashier's window asked for dandelion heads
To hoard for their coarse gold. With this currency
I have acquired a palm tree here, across the fence,
Beyond the Inca daisies which, according to prophecy,
Were transformed to golden rods by the commandment
Of an oracle whose dark voice bade the descendants of the Sun God
To move northward in search of buzzard dollars, double eagles, dough.

Being an entire sunset away, you cannot see this palm tree.
It is luxuriant as a peacock's tail, rainbowed by mist
In the early morning, emerald by starlight. It is not lanky like a giraffe.
Nor is it parched for speech. Hundreds of birds talk in its sixteen storeys.
One day you will race the sun across
America and say: "Why didn't you tell me
About this palm tree that you bought on credit?"
And I will answer: "I told you once when we awoke,
But you have forgotten. Its roots have opened
A savings account in the floating capital of sand that no worm riddles,
Somewhere under the invested asphalt of this marginal soil."

At night,
In the tentative wind, it talks your drowsy lingo,
Its palm feathers whispering of earthquake fluctuations.
I do not know on what stock exchange I bid for it, or
What dividends it should pay, or not pay, annually,
But only that it is gold-edged at sunrise, and that
Its mint par of international exchange is love.

(1966)

# DEDICATED TO *TERRE DES HOMMES*

*Terre des Hommes is a Swiss organization that attempted to arrange the removal of wounded children from Vietnam to European hospitals.*

*Terre des Hommes,* consider how strong your voice is.
I can hear it, far as I am from the glaciers where I once lived,
Yodeling out to those who hang on ropes in the blue crevasses
Or dangle from rock, the cord unraveling swiftly, swiftly.
They are lost in a mountainous and eternal country,
The landscape tight-lipped, gigantic, as they swing, grimacing,
Deaf to the high clear yodel saying: This is the way, this is the way!

(I saw the children dancing in Southeast Asia in August,
Dancing daintily, prettily, with their scarves of napalm,
Their cloaks of phosphorus. These expensive gifts we have sent to them
They will be permitted to keep forever. The opal wings
Of the tissue that once was epidermis contrast so
Effectively with their dark and alien skins.)

*Terre des Hommes,* I hear you calling out that there is time
To return before the last storm whistles down from the north,
Before the ropes unravel to a thread. "In Europe,"
You write on the stubborn snows, in letters as tall
As the palm trees of another continent; "in Europe
We have found several hundred beds." You draw an arrow,
Showing where the Swiss lakes lie, where cows wear garlands
Of gentians around their necks, where children
May rest for a while beneath the ether cones.

(In the jungle of their homeland, no silky tiger moves,
No zebra stamps on the plain, no elephant trumpets, no water buffalo
Ruminates, shifting rice paddy greens between his jaws. Leaves
Have died silently under the stutter of helicopter spray,
And the children, dancing without gas masks, turn toward us
And smile at their own deaths, wondering, but not wishing to intrude.)

For a long time your yodeling went unanswered, *Terre des Hommes,*
Then the word came, written on heavy white paper, white
As the White House. "Dear *Terre des Hommes,*" it began,

And it went on saying: "The American Air Force cannot be used to
    transport the children
Of Vietnam who might be in need of medical attention. There exists
No American financial means to assist your activities.
Yours truly." And the signature? I swear it is not mine.
I wouldn't have had the time to write the letter out. I'm working
Creatively, trying out variations on the theme they dance,
These children who glide through the moonlight, bat-colored now,
Screeching like bats. Their dance cannot be mazurka, not polka,
Not bolero, not hornpipe, or jig. It must be
A regional dance to which they step carefully, carefully,
So as not to disturb the flesh that still clings to their bones.

                                        (1966)

# A POEM ABOUT BLACK POWER

Let us grow old with modesty,
See with our rheumy, failing eyes
That prophets wear cloaks of fire now
(As then). Let us not pound our canes
On the boards for order as we limp across
The blazing stage we knew must blaze.
"Where, where is the red glow spelling 'Exit'?"
Panic cries out; "where, where the asbestos curtain that must fall
Between us and the footlights of our rage?"
Sweethearts, the script has changed (or perhaps not changed),
And with it the stage directions which advise
Lowered voices, genteel asides,
And the white hand slowly turning the dark page.

Let us grow old admitting we saw the fire, the savage betrayed eyes,
Heard the screaming terror of their deaths, and wrote a letter,
Nicely phrased, to someone else, and slept then,
As the old sleep, nodding, remembering. *Remembering what?*
That four little black girls died in a church?
Are we quite certain that we heard their cries?

When they cite Gandhi to you please recall
That he built fires hot enough and tall
Enough to light the whole of India. I was a child then
And, troubled by their flames, each evening knelt and asked my mother
What he burned. "Clothing and rice," she answered,
"Clothing and rice in time of want and famine. Clothing and rice
England had sent in charity to change the look of history,
And did not change it, for Gandhi turned that bribery to flame."

Those fires consumed the debris of my youth,
Burned steadily, burn still, and now I see the lone immortal bird
That wings up from their ash, so clear, so plain.
That the old tremble and tremble and tremble, and cannot say its name.

(1966)

# A POEM IN ONE SENTENCE

*for Clay Putman*

It was more than could have been hoped for
In that lecture hall or theater of the mind crowded
With students in motorcycle dress or else
Bare-legged, feet in sandals, hair amazingly golden,
The boys' longer than the girls'; here, where the tiered
Tilted rows held the restless young (interrupted, as if for comment,
By the weary weary faces of ourselves); it was more
Than could have been expected, your request, tentatively proffered,

That each child cherish a self to which he (or she) might return
When the collective voice had ceased its clamor, that each maintain
A self whose signature did not alter with the season, for
The cheques that history would require that self to put its name to
Would be drawn on another bank (undoubtedly), the currency not the
    same
(As a certainty); requesting that they recall their individual names
Once the outcry here (or anywhere) had died; and if they could not
Answer you then, I promise you they will a long time after,
When their feet are shod, and their hair shorn, each remembering
And answering the request you made in the convocation hall.

(1968)

# FOR JAMES SCHEVILL

*on the occasion of his arrest*

The tongue that serves in courtroom is alien metal,
Having to do with handcuffs, rustproof bars, and interference with activity,
With guilt beneath the nearly annihilated sun, or lack of guilt
Beneath the perishable, soft flowering of apple trees.
Anvilled from one side of the mouth, hot words (like outcry,
Protest, disturbance, felony) are cooled. The courtroom tongue
Clangs "bail, suspended sentence, misdemeanor, own recognizance."
Out of my own recognizance I say the language in which I write
This to you has gone underground; waits as the enduring
Passages of history mingle with the roots of trees, with stones,
With hidden streams. In spring's long sweet conniving,
This language that we sense but do not hear has no alternatives to offer,
Does not acknowledge fear.

In courtroom, classroom, the IBM contraptions shudder. The cold
Of their metal clarions "failed the course," "incomplete,"
"Has not fulfilled the requirements," lacking the range to whisper
"Music" to the uproar. They cannot lift the welded helmets from their
        brows
To see trees fall like executed men. "Metal, metal!" they clang in the
        courtroom;
"Metal!" But in the green leaves of a covert season, poets alone are
        summoned
As witnesses. The fingerprints of poets, blue on file cards,
Speak indelibly of the separateness of man.

(1968)

124

# FOR MARIANNE MOORE'S BIRTHDAY

*November 15, 1967*

I wish you triumphs that are yours already,
And also wish to say whatever I have done
Has been in admiration (imitation even)
Of all you marvelously proliferate. Once someone
Turned to me and said in lowered voice (because you too were in the room)
That William Carlos Williams gave to you at sight that
Singular esteem known by no other name save love. These words were
Spoken perhaps a half century ago
(In Monroe Wheeler's Eastside flat) when you
Wore amber braids around your head. And now,
As then, I cannot write this book or that
Without you. You have always been
Nightingale, baseball fan, librarian of my visions,
Poised on a moving ladder in the sun.

(1968)

# TESTAMENT FOR MY STUDENTS, 1968–1969

Each year you came jogging or loping down that hall
Bearded or not, sweet emissaries from Arizona
Montana, Illinois, Mass., beneath the light silk hair
Or the dark, or the natural crown, skulls crushable, ribs breakable
This year and last wearing sandals in order to run fast
At your temples pools of blood always trembled
And I would see them spill.


Lodged in the red partitions of your hearts
(Where your fathers reigned for a brief time)
On the palpitating thrones of auricle left or ventricle right
Legs crossed, fluently at ease, sat such brothers as Baudelaire
Melville, Poe, sometimes Shakespeare, Genet, Rimbaud; or sisters
Like Dickinson, Brontë, Austin, needlepoint set aside for that afternoon
Or Gertrude Stein telling you over and over how Americans were doggedly
        made
Your fingers, even though broken, crazily beckoned
These brothers and sisters and others to you, in your lungs
Enough breath remained to summon them all by name.
These lines are set down for a reason that's suddenly gone out the window
For I can recall now only your faces: Woodie Haut, Shawn Wong, Rebhun,
        Turks, Alvarado
And how many more. Or I catch now and then the sound of a voice
From a long way away, saying something like: "Poetry is for the people
And it should represent the people." (You can say that again, Woodie)
Or saying: "If the academic poets want to keep poetry for themselves, then
They're no different from the administration of this college
Which wants to keep education for the select few. I am inclined
To agree with Eldridge Cleaver and the BSU that you are part of the
        problem
Or else you are part of the solution." Or maybe Alvarado's voice can be
        heard
Barely whispering under the campus trees: "Don't make too much noise
You might wake up the middle class."


Once I read in a book that the ear of the Oriental records sound so swiftly
So sharply, that the falling of a rose petal from a vase will rouse him

From his sleep. That spring, Shawn Wong awoke to see the mounted police
  charge, yet
It was "the small white flowers trampled in the grass, and the blood
Of poets lying near the broken stems" that stirred his gentle dreams
Or Rebhun will flip aside the armor of arrogance he wears to type on the
  required paper
"If you wish to see mankind, look into the glass. If you look long enough
One man will become ten men, and then a hundred men, and then a
  thousand
We saw the police striking out in a sadly strange fury. Each time
The baton fell on bone, the pain was felt by all of us. For
Behind the physical manifestations of our fervor we are one man
Asking for another world, a world in which we are less tools
Of an impersonal power, and ten or a hundred or a thousand men of flesh
  and blood."

## THE UNGARBLED STORY THAT UNFOLDED BEFORE ME

Well, the incident I want to tell you about came to pass in a college small
enough to put in your pocket. In the northern sticks of California it was,
where a middle-aged white professor got up on the auditorium stage to in-
troduce a black psychiatrist to what was left of a student body scattered in
the seats on a rainy afternoon. The two principal characters had beards, but
no two beards could have been more different one from the other. The black
man's was a handsome addition to his face. The professor's was thin and ail-
ing, but still he had managed to train it to do his bidding. Whenever he
turned his shrunken head, the point of his beard jerked accusingly in still
another direction, indicating with severity that education lay, if you were
only able to see it, in that dusty corner right over there.

"Dr. Parnassus is not just a psychiatrist who is black," the professor began
this memorable introduction. "He is a *black* psychiatrist. I hope you can all
grasp that distinction." For some reason nobody in the audience said:
"Right on, brother" as he stood looking out over the auditorium, his beard
pointing this way and then that. The black psychiatrist himself had in-
stantly become expendable as he sat on the stage fingering his yellow silky
tie. "There are not many around," continued the professor, and this was cer-
tainly the truest thing that had been said that afternoon, for the psychiatrist
was the only black face within a mile or two.

And then the professor turned to the exciting subject of himself. For a num-
ber of years, he said, he had been interested in the problems of minority
groups, and in particular in the black man in the black ghetto. "I say, that's
awfully good of you, old crutch," said somebody out of the top drawer of my
English mementos. ) And now the professor charmed everyone there with
the avowal that he was about to lay the foundation for, or to initiate, or else
to inaugurate, a course at this up and coming institution for the study of a
Black Studies Program, and his beard waved sparsely in the direction of the
psychiatrist. "I hope to have many eminent black scholars come to talk here
on the subject of a study for the development of what may eventually be-
come, we hope," he said.

"Those who have been closely involved in educational procedures," the pro-
fessor proceeded, excluding the audience from that happy experience, "have
established beyond question that there is no possibility of successfully inau-
gurating – or initiating, if you prefer – or, indeed, laying the foundations
for, any course unless that inauguration or initiation has been preceded by a
long term study in depth of what it may be advisable to undertake at some
future time." There was a perceptible movement of restlessness among the
seated, including the psychiatrist, and the professor's beard jerked toward
the door marked "Exit," but no one rose to go. It could have been that no
one in the history of the college had ever got up and walked out in distaste
for what was being said.

The students in this place wore marvelously clean tan Levis, and navy blue
windbreakers. The young men's hair was splendidly trimmed, and the
girls' hair was anything but long and untamed. They all had regular shoes
on their feet. It was another era entirely, and the things the professor was
saying kept carrying us even farther back on the assembly line of his eager
self-esteem. "This is somewhat of a pilot course I am initiating," were his
words. "I might say it took a good deal of personal ingenuity to get it
started, for it has a touch of revolutionary daring about it." (Oh, how
dreary, dreary, can the purveyors of education be if you let them get out of
hand for even two minutes, and this is what had taken place. That's what
rock and roll is for; I knew it with sweet exhilaration then. It's the only thing
loud enough to drown out the voices of the cautious of our day. ) "A pre-
study of a Black Studies Program could scarcely be considered anarchistic
in concept," the professor hastened to add, his beard ready to do battle for
him if it came to that. "Wisdom and reason are not the most popular words
in our current vocabulary, but I still find them useful. This semester will be

devoted to studying with patience and wisdom what reasonable procedure
we can develop which will lead... "

There are times when there is nothing left to do but take a decision, and now
that moment had come. It would have been taken even had the psychiatrist,
after glancing at his wristwatch, not risen to the occasion and made one step
in the direction of the lectern. The professor turned his head in irritation,
and the words died in his mouth. His beard pointed directly to the chair that
the psychiatrist had vacated, but the black man had no intention of sitting
down again. He tapped the crystal of his watch with his long forefinger. "I
have a plane to catch in about three-quarters of an hour. I have to get back to
Watts," he said, and so he was allowed to laugh out loud.

Each year their eyes, midwestern gray or cattle-range blue
Or jet like the ghetto, held visions of what might be achieved
They wrote of the river bank that colonized men slide down
In Fanon's prose, to cleanse themselves of the violence of the dance
Or wrote: "We all sense the pressure of black passion
We lose balance in the presence of the black man's frenzied
Momentum toward autonomy. The urgent tempo with which
He hurls himself at life dazzles us." When I see Victor Turks
Again I'll ask him if he was listening when Sartre spoke
For the dead Fanon, saying that all the inexcusable, the uncondonable acts
Of violence on the part of those at bay are neither sound nor fury
Nor the resurrection of savage instincts, but are part of
The anguished process of man as he re-creates his lost identity
"We should accept the black man's advances toward self-possession,"
	Victor kept writing
Looking up for a moment from *Les Fleurs du Mal, Le Diable au Corps*
"As the means of his salvation. Let *him,* for once, not the white man
Not the European, not Western civilization, but *him* set the example
For us all to follow." It might be in this way, the trembling wind
And the young midwestern voices whistled softly, that we could regain
Our lost humanity. There were many more. There was Father Jim Hietter
Muted laughter, muted grief, melodious student, saying to me
That Christian hate had masqueraded for so long as Christian love
The time had come to call it by its rightful name. "Stuff your holiday
	stomachs,"
He wrote at Christmas. "Paint your world with colored lights

And sleep   sleep   sleep
There is Police on Earth, and Eichmann carols the countdown
To the Christ child's birth."

There were others, among them Chris Miller who bought ankle-high
     sneakers
With air vents, like portholes, near the soles. He loved them so
That he walked with his dark head lowered to watch the pure white
Canvas keeping pace with his thoughts, his talk. "A self
Which does not transcend itself is dead," he said. I see the sideways
Shy, dark smile and the pointed chin. "So let me rise into life
And die naked like an animal, which I am," he wrote, "and be buried
In my mother's earthy body, to rot, and to fertilize the soil. Thus
Death will be my final offering to God."

You were not afraid of death, sweet emissaries from Arizona
Montana, Mass., and Illinois; or of mace, or of handcuffs or clubs
And there's one thing more: you bore the terrible knowledge
That colonized men and poets wear their sharpest pain on the surface
Of their flesh, like an open sore
But this year the writers you honored were, with the crack of a baton
Turned suddenly to stone. Their tongues were hacked from their throats
By bayonets, and the blows came steadily, savagely, on the exquisite
Brittleness of bone. What good were the poets to you then, Baudelaire,
    Whitman
Rimbaud, Poe? "All the good in the world!" you shouted out
Through the blood in your mouths. They were there beside you on
The campus grass, Shakespeare, Rilke, Brontë, Radiguet
Yeats, Apollinaire, their fingers on the pulse in your wrists
Their young arms cradling your bones.

(1969)

130

# FOR JAMES BALDWIN

Black cat, sweet brother,
Walk into the room
On cat's feet where I lie dying
And I'll start breathing regularly again.
Witch doctor for the dispossessed,
Saint tipping your halo to the evicted,
The world starts remembering its postponed loyalties
When I call out your name. I knew you hot nights
When you kept stepping
The light fantastic to music only the wretched
Of the earth could hear; blizzards
In New Hampshire when you wore
A foxskin cap, its tail red as autumn
On your shoulder. In the waters of the Sound
You jumped the ripples, knees knocking,
Flesh blue with brine, your fingers
Cold as a dead child's holding mine.

You said it all, everything
A long time ago before anyone else knew
How to say it. This country was about to be
Transformed, you said; not by an act of God,
Nothing like that, but by us,
You and me. Young blacks saw Africa emerging
And knew for the first time, you said,
That they were related to kings and
To princes. It could be seen
In the way they walked, tall as cypresses,
Strong as bridges across the thundering falls.

                       In the question period once
A lady asked isn't integration a two-way
Street, Mr. Baldwin, and you said
You mean you'll go back to Scarsdale tonight
And I'll go back to Harlem, is that the two ways
You mean?

We are a race in ourselves, you and I,
Sweet preacher. I talked with our ancestors
One night in dreams about it
And they bade me wear trappings of gold
And speak of it everywhere; speak of it on
The exultant mountain by day, and at night
On river banks where the stars touch fingers.
They said it might just save the world.

(1969)

# THE JEWS AMONG THE NATIONS

*for Erich Kahler*

Your sentences cast print and paper to the winds,
Become a crowd so dense there is no parting
Thigh from thigh or man from men, become a tapestry
Of flesh, of human eyes, that fire must shrink from,
Cower before. Your hastening voice describes a temple stone
By stone, a solid residence in which
A tribe, a proverb, an astonishment, may dwell.

Time you define as a long march obscured
By shouting. But time is like a desert where
Your quick acuity dispels the veils of mirage so that one can see
There could have been no trees, no water for the bending reeds,
No reeds, only the semblance of these, and the loose sand
Slipping beneath the vagrant foot of man. You say
That those who drown – whether in water or sand or in their own despair –
Are not effaced, but live in the tribal might of "an invisible
Mysterious deity," changeless and burning, like the pitiless, golden
Gazing of the sun. Those who survive, you say, live singularly apart, elusive
As strangers among other men.

You quote the Babylonian Talmud saying
Of the Jews: "This people has been likened
To the dust, it has been likened to the stars. Sinking,
It is debased to dust. Rising, it is lifted to the stars."
You note the prophecy that the lives of these men shall
Hang in doubt before them all their days, that they shall be given
Trembling hearts, and sorrow of mind,
That the soles of their feet shall know no rest.
These things amaze me that you say.

Your clarity gives the labyrinths a lantern, crosses
Rivers by means of planets, climbs the arid hills of what remains
To man, hastens, hastens, through the centuries, bidding the Jew,
"Self-critical, self-ironical," to enter by the same door,
Pass under the same arch, as the German "arrested and immured"

In national identity, recalling that Jews alone
Inhabit as fluid men the kingdom of a temple built
Within a long astonishment, live in the wisdom
Of a proverb I had not know was there,
Or anywhere.

(1969)

# A POEM FOR SAMUEL BECKETT

I'll not discuss death with you by any name, however gently, soberly, you
    ask.
When the spectacle of it comes downstage, well off-center, "white hair,
White nightgown, white socks," let humor lead the onslaught decked out
In coat-of-mail, broadsword or flash-light in gauntlet, no matter which.
Buckle on uproarious wit, lower the visor so that no convulsed member of
    the audience
Glimpse the whitening eye or lip a-quiver with palsy. Then are we
    authorized to dance,
Hand in clanking hand (though two continents, one ocean intervene);
    suffered to sing,
But not with the voice of mourning dove in the tearful willow grieving,
"Seul, pas seul. Seul, pas seul," but between strophes preening, grooming,
The few remaining feathers of our iridescence, lovely they were — but stop
    the music!
No past tense permitted either here or there.


Maybe, maybe, I say, Krapp speaks (not spoke) for all eternity, his tape my
    tape as well,
And the voice that mysteriously whispers now off-stage asking "what is
    required of me
That I am tormented thus... "? Or saying (whispering still) that the
    humming-bird
Is "known as the passing moment... it comes in from the right" to fly
In a "lightning semi-circle deasil," then comes a shimmering respite, "then
    the next
Then then... " O, words akin to flying bird hum to the tongue at closing
    time
When drink completes its circle, and you neither helping nor hindering me,
Nor lending me your arm as I flounder through the door, chasing the last
    bus
Wending its way up Grafton in the summer dark. Maybe, maybe, I say,
It's the contour of the island that is to blame, the shape of a harp enough
To have caused all the trouble, but no answer's forth-coming; for what
    country
In its right mind, I go on with it, would choose a triangle strung with cat-
    gut,

Or man-gut, finer than rain? It strikes the old notes, plucks the classical
    tune,
The score of seven centuries past, and on into the next one, the music
Ever music. I have promised you not to love the shape of it too well,
Or the men who touch the harp strings of their land with longing; promised
Not to walk Ireland's highways and by-ways without remembering your
    departure,
Not to speak the names Pearse, Connolly, McBride, or to mention their
    valor,
Not to weep my alien tears by Liffey or Shannon. I will look on them
    passing
In the turbulent current, see them in the springtime of what they were
And then in Dublin's winter and Athlone's, but give no sign. I shall hear
Their fists pounding the granite of river-walls and wharfs, the long dead
    stone,
Their faces veiled in mist, warned and bemoaned all autumn by the fog-
    horn of my heart.

2.

No questions, please. The final verdict has been pronounced.
Once the bones no longer boil in the heart's fluid, in that
*Pot-au-feu* of choicest cuts, that quivering stew, know that the fire
Is quenched and the catastrophe of ash is on us. Remnants of a better time
Is what we are, bent, tottering on the brink, gripping canes in our mottled
    claws
To hold the enemy at bay (or, better still, to crack his grinning skull).
"Keep your distance!" we cry out at dawn and dusk. You say you can't go
    on,
And then reverse it, and I follow the change of pace like the finger of a
    metronome,
Calling out to hungering death that there's little nourishment in us,
With even the marrow turned to dust. Instead, riding the gnarled hip-bones
Of skeleton nag, poor, penniless death, or tripping on the curve of his
    reaping, weeping scythe,
Consider the carrots and turnips Vladimir and Estragon have to offer.
These edibles, having pushed up in triumph, waving head-dresses of leaf
    and fern
In the sweet light, they alone have succulence. The weight of dark and
    damp that was their past
Is now our future, we who are plucked instant by bleak instant of our finery,

Stripped of our elegant feathers one by one.
But sometimes, maybe at night-fall, more likely in the dawn of threatening
    day,
When thoughts stampede in panic, hoofing and shouldering aside in the
    barricade of their corral,
Listen a while to the Hedge Row teachers and believe again; give eye and
    ear
To the poets devout among them, young as those other Irishmen who lean
    on oak or zinc
In country pubs, but the elbows of their jackets differing. The weave of
    those
Who sleep on moss or stone is threadbare as spiderweb, and no woman's
    needle there
To embroider the ravelling into cloth again. Or hear one voice keening
That long had been his wandering from far Banaloch to where the outlawed
    sages taught
In the hedges near the waters of Louch Lein; or another, awaking in the
    dew,
Saying he had walked the leather of his shoes away and away to reach the
    sound
Of the music poets spoke in the furtive, lonely lanes, seeking to be guided by
    their lore.
There were no books to open or close, no paper to set pen to, no pen,
Only the melody of speech running from the tongue, the history of learning
Fluid in the sap of the flowering hedge-row, in the silk of the petals,
Their names with the shudder of heartbreak in them, the tuition one potato
    a day.


### 3 · REINCARNATION

There is death in the house.
The spider trapped in the bathtub (slick as a glacier
Its polished heights) is traveler without rope, no thread to unwind, alone
At the end in the slipping and sliding back
Into despair. At the closed pane, the fly curses aloud.
The furtive mouse, steel necklace of trap at its throat.
Is lonelier, greyer, quieter than stone.

May not the process of return to life be so
Reversed that mouse, spider, fly, and even man,

Not having heeded the trilogy of great demands,
Be granted ever higher form until response to what is asked
Is acted out? ("Oh, Jonah he lived in a whale. He made his abode in
That fish's abdomen. Yes, Jonah he lived in a whale.")
And might not fly and spider, mouse and man
Return with the eye of the Blue Whale to offer sight
For the lone search for others of his kind; voyage
Through brine as does the Grey Whale, following seamarks set
Like milestones in the current, gauging the distance to mating
By the stars; return as Bowhead Whale, shifting ice-floes
As easily as scenery in the wings to make a corridor for those who come,
Frolicking, within his spangled wake?

So might transfigured mouse and spider, fly and man
Hear at long last the singing of the Humpback Whale, the arias
Of migration humming and warbling within the ancient flood,
And, hearing, lift on their shoulders a harpooned brother from the tide of
    blood.

4.

*(on the deaths of Roger Blin and Alan Schneider)*

"Hearken," the Pawnee heralds in each stanza. "Hearken."
And I begin this message "hearken" so you will turn your head my way.
"Hearken to fervent vow and anguished prayer," the Pawnee says
In his own tongue, "for each god in his place grants or rejects man's
    suppliant cry."
(Hearken to the stampede of clouds called thunder as if it were no louder
Than the passage of dandelion hair turned white and drifting.)

The Pueblo knows harm is done when guests feast, drink and cry aloud at a
    funeral,
For the priest warns of the hazards if the living mourn over long
Or with excessive lamentation. "As the axe splinters the live tree," he says,
"So the ritual of the hours is sundered by grief. To weep while fires
Go unlit is to question the cycle of the seasons. It is blasphemous
To ask winter to bear guilt for its failure to be spring. Long bewailing,"
He says to the bereaved, "detains the spirits when they seek to go.
Hasten now to sprinkle the road out of the village so that the dust
Lies quiet under their departing feet."

At the ceremony for the dead, the priest speaks of the rites that lend strength
To the living who falter. "As youth departs the hearth for the lonely
Territory of time that lies ahead," he counsels, "so must the spirits
Be set free of the remembrance of the habitual trails. Do not ask the dead
To carry a burden of longing with them, but let them go with steps
As unhindered as the footfalls of spring rain. How can it matter
What we forget and what we remember? Memories belong to the living
And cannot be taken to another place. You have traveled along thorny
      ways,"
He says to the abandoned. "You have passed trees that have fallen in the
      storm,
And those you cherished are fallen among them. Memories wait in ambush.
Take the tumult of desolation from your ears so that the notes
Of bob-o-link and thrush can be heard again. Clear the treachery of dusk
From your eyes so that you can distinguish east from west, north from
      south.
If you go weeping through the forest, how will you find the way? O,
Wrench the iron of sorrow from your throats so that your voices are
      discordant no longer.
Dwell instead on the courage of the dead. They enter a world where they
      will carry
The sun as a shield and learn to use their left instead of their right hands."
O, hearken!

# POETS

Poets, minor or major, should arrange to remain slender,
Cling to their skeletons, not batten
On provender, not fatten the lean spirit
In its isolated cell, its solitary chains.
The taut paunch ballooning in its network of veins
Explodes from the cummerbund. The hardening artery of neck
Cannot be masked by turtle-throated cashmere or foulard of mottled silk.

Poets, poets, use rags instead; use rags and consider
That Poe did not lie in the morgue swathed
Beyond recognition in fat. Consider on this late March
Afternoon, with violet and crocus outside, fragile as glass,
That the music of Marianne Moore's small polished bones
Was not muffled, the score not lost between thighs as thick as bass-fiddles
Or cat-gut muted by dropsy. Baudelaire did not throttle on corpulence,
Rimbaud not strangle on his own grease. In the unleafed trees, as I write,
Birds flicker, lighter than lace. They are the lean spirit,
Beaks asking for crumbs, their voices like reeds.

William Carlos Williams sat close, close to the table always, always,
Close to the typewriter keys, his body not held at bay by a drawbridge of
    flesh
Under his doctor's dress, no gangway to lower, letting the sauces,
The starches, the strong liquor, enter and exit
With bugles blowing. Over and over he was struck thin
By the mallet of beauty, the switchblade of sorrow, died slim as a gondola,
Died curved like the fine neck of a swan.

These were not gagged, strangled, outdone by the presence
Of banquet selves. They knew words make their way through navel and pore,
Move weightless as thistle, as dandelion drift, unencumbered.
Death happens to fatten on poets' glutted hearts. ("Dylan!"
Death calls, and the poet scrambles drunk and alone to what were once
    swift, bony feet,
Casting a monstrous shadow of gargantuan flesh before he crashes. )

Poets, remember your skeletons. In youth or dotage, remain as light as ashes.

# ON TAKING UP RESIDENCE IN VIRGINIA

*for James Joyce*

Here in this territory of state or mind, this precinct,
Bailiwick or diocese of heat and thunder-headed sky, I
Think of one who fled his native soil of church and law and sought
A refuge between hotel rooms, afraid ( as all men fear, and fear, and fear),
Yet drew no academic robe about him, donned no skirt of priest
Against the chill, displayed no metal emblem of his lot, but softly walked
The cool green alien land of what had once been diocese or bailiwick
Of home. That year, he closed the Austrian doors of hotel rooms
( Salzburg it was) against the splintering arrows in the sky, against
The wild black summoning of drums.

The lightning struck timber of barns, dark-eyed cattle, golden hay. In the
    applause of clouds
Colliding no sense to hark to Mozart winging from the *Festspiel* stage.
Pronged fire had ripped the harps to kindling, snapped the taut gut of
    violins;
Sweet warbling tenor, growling bass, and hearty baritone sang on,
    inaudible;
Sopranos shrieked their agony in vain.

Only when the drenched curtain of rain descended did his trembling cease,
And at that ending I reached out to touch the hand of one who now could
    hear,
Not music or the dying clamor of the storm, but rain, the Irish rain,
Come humbly to where he stood on foreign soil; the rain, crying
Its heart out on the Salzburg stones.

# ON THE DEATH OF MY STUDENT, THE POET SERAFIN

Each time a perishable shadow fell
outside the office door
                room 209 Humanities Building
it was you
                the shadow is engraved there now.
The others came
                bearing the cunning subterfuge
of candle tongues that flickered an instant
haloing their greed for praise
                outlined the appetite for self
its endless scribblings on a page
                creative writing the uproarious
                name.

While you at the door
were brother to Chavez
                were and are
a bright-lipped black-crowned sultan in the vineyards
reading poems to bury Marcos by
                            poems to rinse the
                            streets
of far Manila of men and women's blood
                you reading:

        "we lived in a basement on
        divisadero street where

        my grandmother kept her
        colony of immigrants
        together with adobo and
        rice a commune of tangled tongues
        reciting rosaries to father
                flanagan on radio
                station KRAP"

reading until the hour when
the syllables of grief slipped like rain
                    like tears along the wire
strung across the bay
                    one dull as a cinder
among the opalescent syllables of your name
balancing sliding trembling
                    from there to here.

And now the furious ego clamors
to know were the doctors expert agile enough
to scapel a poet's brow
                    the ego stampedes
through the hideous massacre of Serafin
                    sees his flesh
a bruised magnolia flower in the operating room
shouts out I would have entered the lancet
differently into the ivory skull! Not kept
quiet fingers on the fallen petal of his wrist
but beaten the old hawk off
                    with my bare hands
broken like rattling palm fronds
the lone syllable's stiffly feathered wings
                    done more
cracked the hooked beak of death
                    like a blackened walnut shell!

Serafin return
I say return I cry it under the tall campus trees
there are questions I need the answers to:
how many poems were in your veins that night
and did you for a moment recognize
behind the surgeons' masks
the grinning harlequin of death's disguise
                    return return
for the last long paper of the term.

One day sitting in the callous sun
you wrote a poem a joke you named "a takehome final"
                    it began:

"describe your last dream
in your next dream"
and it ended:
"write an obituary using
only four and three letter
words then
till love
dies cry."

# ADVICE TO THE OLD

## (INCLUDING MYSELF)

Do not speak of yourself (for God's sake) even when asked.
Do not dwell on other times as different from the time
Whose air we breathe; or recall books with broken spines
Whose titles died with the old dreams. Do not resort to
An alphabet of gnarled pain, but speak of the lark's wing
Unbroken, still fluent as the tongue. Call out the names of stars
Until their metal clangs in the enormous dark. Yodel your way
Through fields where the dew weeps, but not you, not you.
Have no communion with despair; and, at the end,
Take the old fury in your empty arms, sever its veins,
And bear it fiercely, fiercely to the wild beast's lair.

# BRANDED FOR SLAUGHTER

*for Shawn Wong*

I have been reading, telling people I have not, knowing this
To be a grave illness, this searching and sorting through the words of others
And not one's own. I have read dark truths, such as: hiking over alpine
          paths,
Guides were struck by the scenes of massacre. No longer the blazing blue
Of gentians could be found on the summits; the white felt clusters of stars
Called edelweiss had faded from their galaxies; the dwarf fern shrivelled
To dust; all that had withstood the slashing of winds, the onslaught of rains,
The ice of one century, the crater-hot sun in another season, wasted
Without outcry by the silent footprint of man.
Once cursed by the sophistry of reading, one learns there are places
Named My Song, My Lay, where there were other tramplings, assaults
Upon leaves, stems, delicate roots, small vines with their palms open,
Flora as delicate as the throats of the young, stalks snapped
Like wind-pipes. Niagara grinds the rock to mist, to spume, and the wasp
In autumn is parched to golden dust, writhing a little, then blowing,
Weightless as pollen, into the honeysuckle ditch where children's bodies lie.
The print of man, so vulnerable on sand, tentative on asphalt, shadow fallen
On the forebearing loam, is shaped like a cemetery stone, and on it
The names of the trampled have been inscribed.

2.

I read "collecting I traverse the garden the world," and recognize
The wandering poet, staff in hand, white-bearded, leading others
In the Adirondack dance. I read "here lilac with a branch of pine,"
And see pine and lilac blacken and rot, the garden the world stricken
Beneath the foot of poet, mountain-lover, men terrible in their virtue,
In the simplicity of their crime. "There is no space left for the footprint
Of man," is said no louder than a far plane writing its polluted
Mandate across the sky. Once gone, the hot mouths of flowers will feed
On weightless toads, humming-birds, lizards in coats of mail, rasping
Cicadas. Vine ropes, throbbing like arteries, will vein the continents
With sap; mica and quartz will glitter like planets, and lady-slippers

Dance again where man once tracked down the vegetation, as bison
Were tracked down. The print of man stamped moss back into the rock;
His hand silenced great orchestras of trees, branded for slaughter
The lavish hills. There is no time left to summon pride out of the carnage,
Only the time to turn away without grieving, yes, without grieving,
And to go.

# THE STONES OF A SEVENTEENTH CENTURY VILLAGE

Here in the South of France cicadas rasp, rasp, needles
Stuck in the grooves of August, scraping the measure
For the marching files of caterpillars, dusty accordians
Opening and closing, opening and closing in velvet silence
On their pilgrimage of devastation to the olive trees.

Bleached spears of wheat stand upright in the fields of lavender.
The stones underfoot were once pavings within the massive rock
Of a now vanished house. This ragged path was hallway
Leading from room to room. Now grass lies ashen in the crevices
Of broken steps that women climbed at night to the sound
Of children crying, grass brittle as the hair of women
Who grew old here, the strands still clinging, clawing,
Like the fingers of the drowning, to the parched scalp of the skull.
                    Why am I here in a strange country,
Making my way through the ruins of other women's houses,
Up the abandoned stairways of their soft weeping, while the senseless
        fiddling
Of the cicadas gives no warning of the advance of caterpillars
Through the dust toward the leaves, the trees? Is it because
Of the wheat stalks upright like candles in the lavender, that I cross
The sunken thresholds, calling too late into the dessication
The children's and the women's foreign names?

# A POEM FOR VIDA HADJEBI TABRIZI

## A MAILGRAM FOR BABETTE DEUTSCH

As I write you, discarding for five minutes the names of other women and
    their destinies,
I dismiss as well the vengeance of distance lying between us, valley and tree,
Sierras and Rockies, intervening, and the salt white breasts of Utah
Barricades in the long drift of sand. But have we not called out each other's
    names,
And on some nights transformed the rocky myth of distance into a
    landscape
As light and shimmering as a peacock's open, quivering fan?
It was your poem of the gazelle standing "on legs of matchstick ivory,"
Your grave words saving us at last, saying that each of us carries in her
    breast
A child, holds a child there as the heart is held, anvil and hammer striking
    and striking
Through a lifetime against the bone ribs of its cage. It became
The child in your breast calling out to the child in mine across the distance,
The voice of "the passionate innocent" we had not instructed how to speak,
Crying out to us a total stranger's name. The voices
Of these hidden children summoned her. We had nothing to do with it.
Her steps were silent, as if falling on deep moss, each velvet spear of that
    carpet
Not bleached by frost as where you are, each short, fern-like lancet here,
Under the redwoods, hung with tears of dew; not yours, not mine, but tears
Of a woman who had no further use for them, a stranger to us, who broke
    the crystal string
And let them fall. You sensed her presence when you wrote of "immense
    music"
Beyond a closed and bolted door. She is the music, prison the bolted iron of
    the gate.
Her name is Vida Tabrizi. And there is more.
It comes from Iran, the fierce invocation, not by cable or phone call, not by
    letter or tongue,
But on the fugitive wind that has slipped through the bars. It runs, liquid as
    mercury,

Down the gutters of alien cities, is cried out through the meeting of
    bleeding palms
In the dark. The words of it are broken like flower stems between the teeth.
The message is fearful, the meaning hideously clear.

## THE DECIPHERED MESSAGE

A woman was arrested as she returned home
In the evening. But wait — not a poor woman,
Not disorderly in any way. A young woman, her hair black,
Teeth white, she was seen laughing on that final day.
She was well-dressed (the broad avenues of the residential quarter
Attest to that). She carried a brief case in her hand.
What in the world had she been up to, this woman arrested in Teheran?
They say French and English came easily to her tongue, as well as Middle
    Persian,
But she had been caught committing research, not on rocks
Or the quality of the soil, or on the lava of oil moving slowly,
Slow as a caravan of camels creaking across the desert
On their splayed feet. She had written about peasants,
The conditions of their days and nights. That was it.
Iranian palm trees rattled the indictment, vultures had the nerve
To scream it as they tore at the flesh of the living and the dead.
Hyenas, slope-backed in the throne room, laughed in high C
About it. That's how the royal family came to know.

## THE GEOGRAPHY

Tabriz is a city in Iran, home of the Blue Mosques,
Shaken by earthquakes year after year. Tabrizi is a woman
Who clings with finger-tips turned skeleton-white,
Clings to the edge, and we are the edge to which she holds,
And not quite holds, and falls, yet not quite falls, clinging
To our flesh and bone as though they were her own.
She is the "immense music" you wrote of behind the iron
Of a closed and bolted door. "Tabriz?" the curious ask,
Finger finding it on the map. Tabriz is a city, a place.
Tabrizi is the syllables of both our names.

# THIS IS NOT A LETTER

This is not a letter

    it is not a flask of whiskey to be carried on the hip not wine offered across the table to you it is not voice of any woman speaking in complaint

(too many besides mother wife the small outcry of daughter have already
      spoken
it is now the moment for men to speak)

This is the knell of artists' voices tolling, tolling for one poor painter

    it is the voice of Marcel Duchamp saying

    "Make it clear as the ice of glaciers we once crossed together make it clear that a choice is given is always given

    "tell him that I have been there and chose between being the broken handle of a man or the skeleton of a painter all the bones in place

    "tell him I said a choice is offered but not for long not like a bargain-sale when summer turns to winter this choice is offered maybe once and it is now his hour of decision forty years old the time of man's despair

    "tell him Wols is a handful of chipped marble shattering the windshield of a cop car that Wols is a ripped canvas that can't be painted over forgotten at the back exit tell him there is a front door to walk through if he can see it stumbling drunken in the dark"

This is not a letter

    it is the tolling of voices it is John von Wicht saying

    "I have told him if his hand the precision of it is anything to him if his brain so quick has ears to listen with then he must listen "tell him I have cried tears for him in my bed at night cried for the two men the wrong one the right one tell him I have cried and now I cannot cry anymore for him it makes me sick it breaks my heart"

And now it is Wols's voice shouting from his tormented grave into the silence
"*Ne te détruis pas, imbécile!*"

It is Wols's voice
choked with the dirt of France burned dry by *mille e tre* quarts of lava molten in his blood

saying

"do not tear the curtains from the windows do not puke your heart onto the cobbles and grind it to leather under your black heel do not rock yourself in your arms for solace whispering this is one night only there will be others to retrieve it *ce n'est pas vrai! ce soir est tous les soirs!* each night you rage with is one more passage in a honeycomb of foul decay *je te le dis* women fight over my remains counterfeit pencil gouache oil to sell as mine and I? I am lonely here in the dark take my place for an hour *seulement une heure pour que je puisse chauffer mon coeur au soleil de la vie.*"

# WHAT PARENTS DO NOT YET KNOW

The tree that lingers at the window is just sixteen,
And you, uneasy parent of its wanton ways,
Eavesdrop upon the whispering of three-fingered leaves.

The pale pink squirrel who dances in the nude,
Chattering of nuts, with eyes that see five ways,
Is not related to the tree's anomalies, nor grieves

That you, tormented guardian of bark and roots
And leaves, must seek for words to ratify the pact.
You were once witness to departing wings that fled defiantly

One winter night; hear now the fragile music as it weaves
Like ivy through the cawing of the crows. Not wasp, or cattle ant, or bee
Is hesitant, for each believes his paragon of industry is what
Transforms a tree to a child, and child to tree again ( with softly whispering
    leaves).

# A POEM FOR THE STUDENTS OF GREECE

On the weekend, the upholstery of a sofa was replaced
In the lobby, the gracious lobby of the Acropole Palace Hotel.
A student carried there at dawn had bled to death,
Had bled to death on the brocade. By noon in the lobby,
The classical lobby, where magazines are sold, the marble floor
Had been scrubbed clean of any trace, of any trace. In the lobby
Imported perfumes and foreign papers may be bought, and by noon
The marble was scrubbed clean of the reflection of the dying student's
Face. Athenians and tourists spent the evening at
The usual night-clubs, the customary places, saying —

Saying what?
When street-lights hang by swinging wires
And voices in the dark cry, "Thailand, Thailand,"
What can be spoken of in night-clubs,
In the customary places? When voices
Unacquainted yet with terror call
Their summons from the barricades,
"Parents, join us! We are your children!
We fight the battle for you! Do not let us die!"
What answers can be given in the customary
Places, in the desecrated lobby
Where a student bled to death on the brocade?

"I took life, and faced her," Neruda answers gently;
"And won her, and then went through
The tunnel of the mines
To see how other men live . . .
When I came out, my hands stained
With garbage and sadness, I held
My hands up and showed them to the generals,
And said: 'I am not a part of this crime.'"

We have been told many things, many things,
By the wise, by those who read deeply, deeply in books,
And, reading, perhaps miss the sudden, wild passage of wings
At dusk, miss the white lanterns of magnolia lit on the branch,

The tapers of Bishop Pine trembling before the altar of night,
Miss the blazing of winter cones split open by dawn, and the green,
The unfading green of the olive under its canopy of leaves.
The wise have said poetry explores the landscape of the self,
And the defiant ask if that isolate and lonely territory cannot be
Blighted by drought, without oasis, its single well, its single tree
No more than mirage. The defiant say
The voice that cries "I, I" is dry as a locust's rasping wing.
We are told by those who read deeply, deeply, into books
That time for a poet is a metronome pacing the gait
Of his heart, that uncertain gait, while time
For the writer of prose is a clock hanging on the wall of his century; or told
That prose is a Coney Island mirror, poetry a window through which
Man seeks to see beyond the glass.

             How does one deal with suppositions
                such as these?


Nanos, Maskaleris, where are the words, whether poetry
Or prose, to speak of the Acropole Palace windows facing
The university's green iron gate that hangs twisted on its hinges
After what took place? Is there poetry or prose in any tongue
To say that on the weekend the upholstery of a sofa was replaced
In the lobby where foreign newspapers are sold, to say
By noon of that first day the marble floor was scrubbed clean of any trace?

     "I am thinking of that age to come," Henry Miller
     Wrote for those who have closed their windows, their doors,
     "When men will fight and kill for God...when food
     Will be forgotten...I am thinking of a world
     Of men and women with dynamos between their legs,
     A world of natural fury, passion, action, drama, madness, dreams..."

What role is left to us, what choice? What words
Can we take in our hands to give the shape of bricks, to shape to bricks,
Such as those clawed from the walls of places where learning
Is barricaded; what color the bricks, the vocabulary flung
At tanks, at helmets, into wave after rippling wave of gas

That twists tears from the eyes, wrings eyes from the head?
Now that the bricks are gathered in shallow piles, become
Monuments marking the graves of the young, how can we say again,
In what language: "On the weekend, the upholstery of a sofa
In the lobby was replaced, and the marble floor scrubbed clean
Of any trace"?

> There are men who seek to look
> Through the window of a poem of their own making,
> Gaze raptly there until the glass clouds with their breath,
> Leaving only the inner landscape of despair. Lew Welch was one
>> who,
> Before shattering the pane, turned back from death to say:

>> "Poets carry the news, they warn the prince,"
>> And asked of us who could not answer:
>> "Has nobody said out loud
>> Our job is to give ourselves away? That
>> Now and then we must rest from that work?
>> That this is the resting-place?"

Ritsos, poet of Greece, poet of prison, poet of house arrest,
Answers the questions about the sofa, the lobby, about the clock,
The metronome, answers Lew's question about resting from the job,
Answers the tanks, the tear-gas, the young dead, saying:

>> "They sit transfixed high in their outposts
>> . . . scanning the tormented ocean
>> Where the broken mast of the moon has sunk.
>> They have run out of bread, exhausted their munitions.
>> Now they load their cannons with their hearts.
>> So many years besieged by land and sea
>> They have starved, they have been slaughtered,
>> Yet none has perished.
>> High in their outposts their eyes shine . . . "

> (Salonika and Athens 1973,
> Revised November 20, 1975)

# A POEM FOR
# THE TEESTO DINÉ OF ARIZONA

The mountain is old. They say she is a female mountain.
The women who know her are not young, yet they call her
The Mother. She stands tall against the sky, fragrant with herbs,
Embellished by shrubs. The mantle that falls from her shoulders
Changes color, tree-shadow by shadow, as it drifts to the valley,
Changes texture in slope after slope of grain. Her earrings
And rings are shrines for the healing ceremonies. Offerings
Of turquoise, abalone, jet, coral and white shells are brought
To her now, as in other centuries, gifts for the Holy People
Who live in her veins. She is The Mother who stands in silence
When the land is fettered and barbed with wire, when it is parched
To dust by the drought of uniformed men.

     ( Take a look at Mr. Relocation
     As he comes dancing, prancing
     Up the pike, cha-cha-ing to the music
     Of hidden coal in the Mesa, comes hushing
     The blare of the bugles of uranium, finger
     On lips, duet of handcuffs at his belt keeping time
     With the intricate steps of his macabre dance. )

What can be said, or written, or cried out to Roberta Blackgoat,
To Ruth Bennally, to Pauline Whitesinger, whose lives
Have been lived at Big Mountain, who graze their cattle there?
"When the time comes, if we don't have any choice," is what Ruth Bennally
    is saying,
"We'll fight with our fists." They have seen the trespassers come
To garrote the ceremonial hogans, dynamite the sacred springs.
"When I fired," is what Katherine Smith says, "they were fencing
Right across the wash from my home. Indian police came to arrest me.
I told them they couldn't. They were my sons, the same blood
Was running in our veins. Only a white man can arrest me, was
What I told them. So the white men came and took me away."
And Pauline Whitesinger whispers: "They can shoot me standing here
In my bare feet. I won't put shoes on for them," her voice
Quiet as the foot-fall of a deer.

("Relocation" is the word, the death sentence given
To people with another look in their eyes,
To those with the beaks of eagles, who carry
Their history with them as they go. It is a word
For the uprooting of trees, for the turning to stone
Of sap under city streets, for the harnessing
Of deep rivers in a ravished land.)

In Flagstaff, prayers cannot be offered to Big Mountain.
In Flagstaff, the medals and uniforms speak of other things.
But far in the dark, thunder shouts down the long impounding:
Impounding of the singular music of ore in the hills,
Impounding of the slumber of coal, impounding, impounding;
Far in the dark, trees grieve aloud in the wind,
Bemoaning the long enduring of the Cherokees' Trail of Tears,
The Navajos' Long Walk of their despair. In the dark,
Horns of lightning rip wide the night. Oh, believe me, believe me,
There will be more in the end than the labyrinths of rusted wire
And the empty tear-gas cannisters left on the trampled grass.

# POEM FOR A PAINTER BENT ON SUICIDE

You drive a hard-nosed, ungelded bargain
With the times. You demand the last penny
Be paid in full, even though broken like a heart
Or colt. Can you accept this fiscal year
As a loan I offer (at exorbitant interest),
To be repaid over the legal interim required
For cancelling death? (Or will you choose
To slash with the artist's savage brush "no funds"
Across the canvas of your self-portrait's face?)

Is there a music in the means men take
To file their bankruptcies? Is it done
In any tongue as modest as poetry is,
That *compte rendu* in which the deficit to leap,
Or hang, or sever is written savagely in red?

This autumn accept the last half of April,
Deposited to your account in perpetual
Annuity, the balance to be paid in green-backed
Summer days and currency of nights in silver change.
All this to be kept in safe deposit tins within a vault,
Beneath the tick-tacking of the hearts of lonely men
Who feared not auditor or poetry's devaluation
When they chose to die, but something less:
The forgery of their embezzled faces in a shattered glass.

# A POEM FOR FEBRUARY FIRST 1975

*for Jessica Mitford*

Glance back four years (yes, nearly four years now,
No matter how close, how shuddering the grief). Glance back
To the bonfires, to the curve of the moon lighting the walkways, the
    catwalks,
Lighting the faces of those who stood, arms locked, black links of a chain
Twisting motionless through D-Yard, a barrier of men, alive still
But rigid as the dead. That September the white horns of the moon and the
    bonfires
Shone for a moment in the lonely caverns of their eyes.

Hear the far clang of the syllables: Attica. Do not let them
Slip through the crevices of history, geography, be effaced from
The miraculous ledger of the stars. Say that a civilization was lost here,
Near to a city named for a dying species, Buffalo, not in that other Attica
Leafed delicately with quivering olive trees, washed on two sides by the
    Aegean Sea,
A triangle of ancient Greece refreshed by small, blue, brimming harbors,
Touched gently by the south wind as it passed. The heights were
Violet-crowned, the fields sweet with jasmine, the townships
Of ancient Attica bore the names of various plants and trees.
Its people are said to have walked gracefully through the luminous
Ether of its dusks. (Why not, with no irons at their ankles, no shackles
At their wrists?) That Attica overlooked the plain of Marathon,
Descended rock by sunbleached rock to the bright pulsing sea.
*Do these things matter now?*

The men locked arm in arm in the Attica of our dust, our maggots, our
    dereliction, stand
Halted at the edge, high on their hushed precipice, men whose names we
    have since learned,
Who choked, who wept, who fell on their knees in D-Yard as the helicopter
    dipped
And let its cargo of gas drift, lazy as smoke, quiet as cloud formations,
Across the rainy dawn. It is said that in ancient Attica
Torch-light processions descended from Athens, rejoicing, and turned the
    coastline

Radiant, fanned the dark harbors into waltzing light. *What torches can we carry,*
*Lit by the dry kindling of our hearts?*


At the first burst of rifle fire, those whose stark names we have since learned
Were mowed down like grain, their blood darker than poppies lying, dying,
In the wheat, and the single curse, "Rockefeller," cut deep in the curve of
each bullet
That scythed them down. Down, down the walkways the assault units
Advanced in their curtain of fire, their cloaks of flame, came in yellow rain-
gear,
In beetle-eyed masks, elephant-nosed, without ears, so that the pounding
On doors was silence to them, the pounding of fists at humble doors where
The locks broke, the wood split wide to the knocking, the knuckles of lost
men
Beating at Rockefeller's door, inmates, hostages, pounding all night,
Pounding into the dawn like taps sounding at the barrier of his grinning
door.
'If he had come, showed that he cared,' whispered the ashes of the
extinguished fires,
'Things would have been different. Men would have lived who had not
asked to die.'


As one approached ancient Attica, it is said that a change of temperature
Could be perceived, a softening of the breath of the wind, of the wash of the
sea.
That Attica was famed for its marble (not for its blood), marble
astonishingly white,
Astonishingly blue; famed as well for the brittle charcoal of its fuel.
(Charcoal obtained from bones is called 'bone black' in the trade.
It lay on the pavings of D-Yard after the fires were done and the pounding
ceased on the stone
Of one man's door.) 'If he had come it would have shown . . . ' whispered
the blowing ash.
But does not stone hold echoes in the hollow of its hands, echoes
That call forever down the corridor of history, across the congregation of
the years,
Calling that all we can know of our own lives is learned
Through the despair of men whose names are not our own?
Remember the word Attica. Remember its syllables clanging, clanging.
*Do not let them go.*

# AFTER THE EARTH QUAKED

*to the memory of Emanuel Carnevali*

After the earthquake, a phenomenon of quiet
Spread, avocado-green, across the land,
The voices of trees still hushed
By the upbraiding of the dark earth's shuddering.
Birds had taken it well; pictures were straightened
In houses; no cracks veined the walls,
No garden gate hung unhinged by
The disturbed slumber of the daffodils; all this
Under the untroubled gaze of distant planets
And lesser stars. The Italian poet, Carnevali,
Once wrote: "The earthquake has little fingers.
You can find the truth in this
In the falling of tiny bits of plaster from the walls."

This morning, he would have written in the reign of quiet
That the earthquake was God clenching his trembling fist
To threaten man on the highways and by-ways of all he had
Become. He would have set it down again: "Hesitating
Everywhere, hesitating fearfully, the few poets, they who weigh
With delicate hands, walk on the unfrequented roads,
Meandering, crying and laughing against the rest."

# TO A PROUD OLD WOMAN WATCHING THE TEARING DOWN OF THE HURRICANE SHED

You did not see wood blackened by rot, or rust-emblazoned iron,
Or gutter riddled like a cabbage leaf. No, none of these.
Not jagged flower-pot, tile without echo, table without leg, or chair bereft
Of arms, or planks striped with mildew like a zebra's hide.
Each board they fed the flame, bepearled with slug, viscous
With writhing worm, remained for you bleached timber of another year,
Crowned with lacy green, forever tree, within the static of your memory.

But there in the old shed's dying your youth died, mourned only
By the turtle-doves this spring. The child and girl and woman named
    Felicity
Watched by the strong sea-wall in separate agonies; the breasts, limbs,
    lovely cranium of all you were
Consumed at last, and through clenched teeth you cried your hideous name.
Yours were the entrails twisting in the flame, the life of all you were to be
Dragged, screaming, from the shed's long dying, ash now with the poems
    not written,
Grace not said, blowing at evening to the dead-end of the driveway's
    ending.
This was a devastating of the past you could not countenance. It brought
    you to your knees
That night under the pale tears of the dogwood's drifting leaves.

But there have been other executions, fiercer, bloodier. There have been
More savage dramas played, when the rope of terror tightened on the throat
And the neck jerked, broken like the heart, your hand nor any other lifted,
    and no requiem sung.
Think of these others now that the last, radiant embers of the shed are dust.
Not for long does the high wind of life take words we speak
From out our mouths, and bear them swiftly, clearly through the air
So that the living and the murdered dead may hear.

( Let it be courage that our tongues compose,
There being no refuge from the hurricane that blows. )

# DECEMBER 1989

*a poem for my beloved Dr. Thomas Stone*

Dear Tom:

T om, I will do anything you recommend
                              and do it
H appily, without protest or argument,
O n the crucial subject of my
M yriad geriatrical infirmities.
A s an example, I would walk at least
S eventy times eighty miles a day

S hould you advise it, or dance all night on
T he head of a pin, as it is said the angels do;
O r leap like a gazelle through hoops of fire,
                              if that were
N ecessary; or sing like a nightingale when
                              bullfrogs croak as
E vening falls upon the marshlands; and chastise the willows who
                              weep at dawn of day.

                    Sincerely,
                    Kay

# A LESSON IN ANATOMY

*We are the descendants of a line of primates bred for competition with one another.*
PETER ALESHIRE

I

The anomalous structure of the inner ear has been designed as
Conduit for the assault of varying chorales of resonance
That skirmish for entry into the red-veined hollows of the skull.
The inner ear of *Homo erectus* (and conceivably of *Homo habilis* as well)
Was not morphologized for words, for there were none. That ear
Was helpless recipient of howl and hoot, cackle and bray, of thunder of
    storm, splintering
Of tree and general hue and cry. In the anatomical history of the ear
There is no evidence either inner or outer was ever equipped for speech.
    (Unlike
The serpent or the asp, it has no tongue.) It cannot billow in menace
Like the ear of elephant or stand erect in fealty or swift alarm, or
Flatten in animosity or fear as have the ear of dog and horse, cat and hyena
Since time began.

II

The semi-circular canals that twist and turn within the cranium of
Modern man have been established as the designated means by which
All messages from without are carried, garbled or not, to the
Uneasy brain. They wind a tortuous way around blockades of pressure
From the heart, glaciers of hardening arteries, lacerating nerves
(For these abound), canals that are submissive to the electro-biological
Current of hammer, anvil and stirrup that modulates all sound.

III

The threshold of the outer ear, known as the lobe, is pierced
At times with silver-plated metal or with brass, at times embellished
By semi-precious jewels that glitter and gleam and brazenly invite
All passing whispers to come in. (O, ear, beleaguered ear, turn deaf
To the maledictions until the fury of the dialogue has been – what?

Has been "exchanged for"? No, no, and also not "transformed to" – O, ear
   do not
Dispatch the unyielding tidings to the brain! Not until – until – What is the
   word
I cannot find? Is it enough to say do not listen to prosecution or defense until
A plebiscite of other voices travels, rejoicing in the verdict, to the brain
And the leaves of poplar trees lie quiet on the branch and the storm asks
Pardon of the gently falling rain? )

( 1 9 8 6 , revised  1 9 9 0 )

# A POEM ON GETTING UP EARLY
# IN THE MORNING (OR EVEN LATE
# IN THE MORNING), WHEN ONE IS OLD

Wake, yes, wake (the Irish have a grimmer meaning
For the word and – so like the Irish – magic the verb
Into a noun.) Yes, wake and cross the Bridge of Sighs
Into the menace of the day. The buckling knees
Betray the thighs and hammer toes reduce their size,
Outraged that they are called upon to stride. "Fall, fall,"
The ankles urge, eager to sprain or to be sprained while,
Whether it rains now or has just rained, Tom's voice
Across the wire decrees that one must walk at least
Two miles a day; also that this pill or another be ingested
(Furosemide or Lasix) on "arising," seemingly unaware that
Rising in the morning is the final chapter of despair.

As the curtain of fog descends (instead of "rising"), bull-frogs
Take on the operatic roles of tenor and baritone, their voices
Hoarse and the libretto lost in the morass. Useless to care
Whether or not the willows cease their weeping
As they braid and unbraid their long green tangled hair.

(April 6, 1990)

# WEATHER

Cruel, cruel is the presence of weather,
Now taking the wind from one's sails then
Flinging it back like a tattered scarf.
Weather is known to have parched and savaged crops
That were green as Ireland is, uprooted and throttled them
For the pleasure of hearing men's hearts break
In two. Weather lashes salt waters into a frenzy,
Severing man and ship from their separate destinies.
With two flips of its tail it will level ant-condominiums,
Tail-winds being its vengeance and its pride. It lures
Butterflies too soon from the silk of cocoons in order to shred
Them with early frost; rips red and gold leaves from bush,
Bough and vine, and stamps them into dust.

Oh, cruel, cruel is the perfidy of weather. In the sunniest hours
Of day it hurls avalanches like waterfalls down mountain heights,
Howling with laughter as death thunders on man and beast below.
And never a tomb-stone marking where they lie.

(April 1990)

# A LETTER TO ARCHIBALD CRAIG

*after the death of Ernest Walsh*

### I

There is one country and no shame to it
For having a heart hot in the breast
And songs in the mouth that servant-girls sing
To their dishes. Wherever the men of that country are,
Are the laughter and the abandon of their land,
And whenever a stranger speaks it is empty words
That he murmurs.

Whether it is that I am deaf now
Or whether it is that I am blinded
And stricken dumb by the thought of the dead,
I am weary, weary for speech like green grass
In the river. I am groping in the dark for the presence
Of him for whom my tears fall.

### II

I ask more of this season of mourning than leaves seeking the ground
Or birds guiding the wind south or a doorstep swept clean
As a tombstone for winter. I ask more than the fingers of stars
Pointing out foot-steps on the wet grass, or the moon ringing the hay-bells,
Or frogs gulping in concert the memory of what was once said.

There is no answer from fields silenced by frost
When there should be a new season blooming, a new history
Written of feast-days, of celebration for a young man
Who died one autumn night.

### III

If I thought this is the way I'd be waiting
When the door opened to let him in,
Locks of hair would be blown on the room's face

And I'd be combing them back behind my ears
If I thought he'd be suddenly there in the glass
This is the way my legs would be crossed and my hands
Lying still if I thought I could see him make sugars fly
By sleight of hand up his cuffs after dinner or magic
Bright coins from the dog's patient ears if I thought
I could hear the music of his steps on the gravel
This is the way my eyes waiting and my heart
Crying until I be dead with him.

# ODE TO A MAINTENANCE
# MAN AND HIS FAMILY

Renato O. Jones, you maintain my beliefs
And service my thoughts when they cease to function.
You repair the ailing equipage of the present, transform
The past into flowers around the shuffle-board court
Where there were none before. You speak
The melodious languages of countries that bask
In the sun, employ vacuum respirator as though
It were rod or staff from the garden of Paradise.

You anoint windowpanes with Windex and kneel
In concern for stains on the carpeting,
As men knelt in ancient cathedrals where their voices
Murmured in prayer. You restore me with dance-steps
From harbors you knew: Shanghai, Marseilles, Trinidad,
And how many others. The songs that you sing
(As you unclog drains or retrieve lights when bulbs
Flicker and fail, or weave copper patches into the webs
Of damaged screen doors) are magical with the music
Of names of your family: Carmelita, Christopher, Dissere,
Alex and Mark, and Kevin and Kenneth and Kerwin.

Each day you say to me — not in words but in the eloquence
Of your presence — that infinite patience with mankind is everything.

(Aug.–Sept. 1 9 9 0 )

# THE CROW

The crow sits in the pine tree
And speaks of many things,
Among them his B.A. and his M.A.
And his Ph.D. He rebukes the gulls
For the grace of their waltzing
      when they come inland
Fleeing from storms at sea.
Dressed in the outfit
      of an undertaker, he lectures pigeons
On their promiscuity, condemns wild geese
For their migratory ways and,
Wrapping academic gown about him,
Flaps off to carve his utterances
      farther, wider,
On the heretofore unsullied air.

(Nov. 1990)
(by Kay Boyle and Ian Franckenstein)